Rodney Plunket

I AM
This Is My Name

by

George A. F. Knight

WILLIAM B. EERDMANS PUBLISHING COMPANY
GRAND RAPIDS, MICHIGAN

Library of Congress Cataloging in Publication Data

Knight, George Angus Fulton, 1909–
I AM: this is my name.

1. God—Biblical teaching. 2. Christianity and other religions.
3. Eschatology. 4. Jesus—Person and offices. I. Title.
BS544.K55   1983   231   83-1585
ISBN 0-8028-1958-3

Contents

Abbreviations

AV   Authorized or King James Version
NEB   New English Bible
RSV   Revised Standard Version
TEV   Today's English Version or Good News Bible

Introduction

A NEW SITUATION HAS DEVELOPED IN RECENT YEARS IN THE area of the relationships between the world's religions. Till recently Hinduism was to be found in India, Buddhism in Thailand, Islam in the Arab countries, and so on. But in one generation, since the end of World War II in fact, all this has changed. As a result of the speed of communication that we now enjoy, and especially through the blessings of television, we have all been drawn closer to one another. Vast numbers of refugees are moving about the face of the earth. Emigrés from the deceased European empires in Africa and Asia now seek their home in the West. The Gastarbeiter of the postwar period in Europe have now settled down as permanent citizens. Consequently, the old inborn notion that "East is East and West is West, and never the twain shall meet" has been shattered seemingly once and for all. Today many Zen Buddhist Japanese live in the United States; thousands of "Christians" live and work in Saudi Arabia; tens of thousands of Sikhs and Hindus live in Manchester, Los Angeles, and Toronto; and even greater numbers of North African Muslims live and work in the cities of France.

The study of the religions of humankind till not very long ago was the prerogative of scholars in Europe's universities. These learned men and women found that they had to travel great distances in order to discover "specimens" of the religion they hoped to study, just as botanists made lengthy expeditions into the mountains of China or into the forests of the Amazon to collect "specimens" on which to write their learned works. Today, however, we grow the orchids of the Amazon in our hothouses and the azaleas of China in our gardens, and these exotic plants now clamor for room to grow and develop in competition with our native wild cowslips and our old domesticated cottage garden hollyhocks. And so it is with man's religions.

It would be wise for us to look at this new phenomenon—not in general, as they used to do in the university classroom, but in particular situations, such as those we experience in our cities now. John Hick has ably done this in his important statement *God Has Many Names* (Macmillan, 1980). Here he pinpoints the bewilderment of the old inhabitants of one particular city that he knows well, namely, Birmingham, England, at the new situation with which they are faced. For the newcomers to that old industrial city have brought with them their various religions, and they are now practicing them seriously and with deep conviction before the eyes of those whose whole way of life had been rooted in what they were pleased to call, or took for granted to be, the Christian Faith.

The first major Christian thinker to interpret Christianity as one religion among others was Friedrich Schleiermacher. He is thus the father of the type of courses that are very popular with students in our Western universities and which are called "Comparative Religion," "The Phenomenology of Religion," and the like. This is the "in general" approach we mentioned. But the "in particular" approach holds together a series of specific issues. For example, in the Birminghams of this world it is particular people, believing in their particular religion, who meet with particular people of other faiths. Again, the word "religion" does not occur in the Bible, except once in the KJV, where it is wrongly rendered. Thus we cannot accept without further examination the dogmatic statement that Christianity is one of the religions of the world. Furthermore, it is particularism that prevents Jesus from being part of a pantheon. He is not comparable with other "divine men"; rather he is comparable only with the God of the Old Testament.

So in the particular situation of Birmingham we find large numbers of Sikhs ("and they never appear in public without their turbans, even when riding motorcycles!"), Hindus (the smell of whose cooking can offend Christian nostrils quite a distance up the street), Muslims (who refuse to eat meat killed in a "Christian" way), and others too, from Japan and Korea and Kenya and Viet Nam. All of these base their customs on the "religion" they claim as theirs and through which alone they give meaning to life in their strange new environment.

John Hick tells us how he studied the faiths of Asia firsthand by living in India and thus coming in close contact with some of those religions. Now he is concerned for those very people in the great city of Birmingham. What they have done by settling in it is to produce a pluralism of faiths where Christian society has never known of such a thing before. The fact of this pluralism, however, has forced him to examine his own faith—his own "orthodox" Christianity, as he honestly declares it to be. He has been compelled, he tells us, to rethink especially the meaning of the Incarnation, that is, the meaning of the relationship between the Jesus of the Gospels and the living God. Moreover, he has done so in fellowship with other sincerely probing and like-minded Christian scholars. They are virtually the same group who some years ago produced that composite volume, *The Myth of God Incarnate*. This work occasioned much controversy when it first appeared. Many agreed with it, and many disagreed. Now John A. T. Robinson, one of the contributors, has added to the ongoing debate his new volume, *Truth Is Two-Eyed*.

I would suggest that the shock occasioned by this new pluralism has produced at least three different reactions within "Christendom." (1) The Christian theological liberal seems to rely unconsciously on the witness of Plato and the philosophers as he seeks to make his answer. (2) The evangelical scholar seems unconsciously to accept that he should think out his Christian apologetic by taking the witness of the New Testament and particularly the person of Christ as his starting point. Yet we should note that the Bible totally rejects all the subtle blandishments of Hellenism, and it does not begin its witness with Jesus and the New Testament. It begins what it has to say "in the beginning."

(3) We are left then with the "average man in the pew" who asks himself whether the differences between his

religion, which may mean very little to him, and that of his "colored" neighbor, reveal anything more than just differences in cultural values arising from history and from geography. So the conversation over a beer in the local pub runs to a dogmatic statement that "there is really no difference between Christianity and Hinduism or Sikhism, for we are all going the same way." This means, of course, that if all religions are "the same," none of them can possibly offer the whole truth. Thus any attempt to be a Christian in our modern society is really not worthwhile and should be abandoned, for we are now living in a "post-Christian" world.

I have no intention of challenging John Hick and his friends by offering a controversial, and therefore probably indignant, reply to the issues raised in his important volume. Indignant answers are certain to be lopsided because they attempt to controvert an issue by means of a tour de force. Rather, what I hope to do here is to make a completely different statement. It is, in fact, that the God of the Bible has only one name, that name by which he made himself known to Moses more than three thousand years ago, namely, *I AM: this is my name for ever*. I believe that unless the Christian gets his theology right he should not enter this area of "The Christian Approach to the Religions of the World"; and he must work at his theology in the particular situation of close friendship with those of other faiths.

I AM:

This Is My Name

CHAPTER 1

The New Birth of the Human Spirit

DURING THE SIXTH CENTURY B.C. THERE WAS A GREAT movement in the spirit of man. It took shape in the many areas of the earth that were then occupied by civilized man —Europe, the Near East, India, and China. It was in the period between 550 and 450 B.C. that most of the great religions and philosophies of the world were born. Before that strange century opened, man's spirit had of course wrestled with the mystery of life and had sought to regularize in terms of religion what it meant to live out the human span on earth. Such a search for reality took place in ancient Mesopotamia and early Egypt, as well as in old India even before the days of Moses, and then again, some centuries later, before Homer. India, obsessed by its existential problem of endemic poverty, pain, and suffering, was seeking, as man must seek, for a meaning in human life that might coordinate all its mysteries and empower humankind to accept the challenge of the world's pain. But now a new era dawned, an era when all over the world charismatic individuals arose and became the founders of world religions. These all held in common the basic view that there can be but one God. Thus no matter by what name we may call him, no matter under how many forms we may think of him, that great God has indeed expressed himself to human understanding.

Gautama Buddha was born about 560 B.C. and died some 60 years later. The son of a *Sakya* from the warrior class, the next-to-the-top level in Hindu society, he turned away from all the privileges that his caste offered; for these merely contributed to his weariness of spirit. He left wife, home, and child in search of such enlightenment as would raise him from

1

black despair to sublimest hope. What he was in search of was peace of soul and certainty of mind. Eventually, as he believed, he received a revelation of the Truth. He became the Buddha, the Enlightened One. He taught that there are four noble truths that must be understood. The first was the fact of suffering (the reality that had crushed the spirit of Hindu India for centuries before). The second was that the cause of suffering lay in man's craving for satisfaction and gratification as well as for power in this life, to which may be added his thirst for a life beyond death. The third noble truth he taught was that suffering must be annihilated, and this can be accomplished by destroying all human desires. The fourth truth was that this goal can be reached by way of "right vision, right thoughts, right speech, right action, right livelihood, right efforts, right mindfulness, and right concentration," attitudes that together cover the three main avenues of human activity—body, mind, and speech. According to his teaching, he who understands these four noble truths has reached the state of *Arhat*. He is the perfected disciple, and has reached the Middle Path between the two extremes of sensualism and asceticism; and so, when death comes, he will enter *Nirvana*, the state of perfect blessedness in which the soul is finally absorbed in the peace of the infinite.

Confucius, in what was even then the ancient civilization of China, flourished almost the same time as Buddha (550–479 B.C.). He gave that vast land a regularized way of moral living that has lasted right till this day. So long ago, then, he recognized that man is a social and political being; and by using a question-and-answer method with his disciples, he established those principles which the "perfect gentleman" should display in his social relationships—"kindness, sincerity, graciousness, loyalty, and self-denial." His philosophy, therefore, was simple: "Virtue is the foundation of happiness."

The Vedic period of **Hinduism** in India had already lasted for a millennium and a half when our "strange period of renewal" in the world's history occurred. Now began that Renaissance of religion in India which brought into being the Hinduism we know today. It was the period when the two great Hindu epics, the *Ramayana* and the *Mahabharata*, began to take their present form. These expound the principles of the ancient *Vedas* by interpreting the exploits of such heroes as *Rama* and *Sita*, who depict the ideals of moral and social behavior for the individual, the family, and the nation. The *Bhagavad-Gita* ("Song of the Lord") calls for doing one's duty in a disinterested manner according to one's status in society. Behind all such moral living is *Brahman,* the one, abstract, all-pervading Reality. All reality in the *Upanishads,* including the self (*Atman*), is an aspect of *Brahman.* The physical world with its apparent diversity is neither real nor unreal; it is mere illusion (*Maya*). "An invisible and subtle essence is the Spirit of the whole universe. That is Reality. That is Truth. Thou art That."

Popular Hinduism is not easy to define. It embraces within it scores and even thousands of gods. Buddhism, in its original form, is almost nontheistic. So also is *Jainism.* Founded by Mahariva, it, too, comes from our strange period, and is an outgrowth of Hinduism. Jainism stresses the doctrine of *Ahimsa,* or nonviolence to all living creatures. It emphasizes stern asceticism in order to conquer the appetites of the body. Like Hinduism in general it believes in the immortality of the soul but emphasizes the transmigration of the soul in particular.

We are not sure of the exact dates of **Zoroaster,** but he, too, flourished in our "strange period." He taught his doctrine of a supreme being whom he called *Ahura Mazda,* the God of goodness and of light, who alone is worthy of worship. But the whole basis of his faith was that Reality is to be understood in terms of dualism. Thus, opposing the God of goodness and light is the God of evil and darkness, *Ahriman.* However, in Zoroaster's system monotheism prevails, and even in the realm of human behavior, that is, in ethics, dualism is not the final answer. In the end, the "Wise Lord" will vanquish the spirit of evil.

The gods of the **Greeks** are as old as Greek civilization itself. But it was in our "strange period" once again that the religious ideas of old began to be explained in terms of mythology. In the old popular piety the gods really existed, living like enlarged human beings on the top of Mount Olympus. But the philosophical genius of the Greeks that showed itself particularly between 500 and 300 B.C. through both its thinkers and its poets revealed the special genius of that people by the way their writers handled their heritage. What they did was to throw their own human emotions and foibles into the sky, so to speak. They took the tales of the ancient gods and turned them into living allegories of what takes place within the human psyche. They used the characters of the gods to interpret the meaning of *human* life, in that for them "man is the measure of all things." So they employed their inherited mythology to create the sciences of psychology and anthropology. They were thus the supreme exponents of the thesis, much trumpeted today, that man creates his gods in his own likeness.

The above sketches are not meant to be examinations of the religious movements of the period from 550 to 450 B.C. For one thing these movements were not all "religious." Some of them emphasized the ethical side of human life, some the political, some the spiritual. We have outlined their tenets here only to make them act as foils to another movement that took place in the 500's, one that was of a totally different nature from any and all of them. This unique "other" movement was not the creation of any human mind, but was a corporate interpretation of historical fact. This interpretation, of all the religions of the world, is alone based on fact. During that period of the second half of the 500's an unknown "voice" made an interpretation of the historical events through which he had now lived. This interpretation is so strange, so utterly different from the thoughts of any other human being at any time in history, that the reader is compelled to ask whether it does not actually come from the mind of God and is thus in the nature of revelation. Man can write about and teach how man can and does control both pain and his natural instincts. Man can describe what it means to live in society as a perfect gentleman should do. Man can describe the many paths that lead upward from the human ego to the area of the divine; in fact, one can even turn inward to meet the divine through the window of one's own belly button, or practice yoga, or follow some human Messiah, whether he comes from Lebanon, Korea, or California. But now we are turning neither to speculation nor to philosophy and ethics, but to history.

The historical fact with which we are concerned was the fall of Jerusalem in 587 B.C. This fall meant not only the total destruction of the city, but also the end of the dynasty of David, the desacralizing of Israel's worship now that Solomon's Temple was no more, the annulment of the moral law that Moses had brought the people centuries before, in that the Decalogue ("written by the finger of God"), which had been incised on stones and housed in the Ark within the Temple, had disappeared now for good, and many other things. Above all else, these events shattered Israel's belief that her God had made a covenant with her that was to last forever. For the "end" of Jerusalem meant exile for "God's people Israel," who would live thereafter as mere displaced persons and no longer as a political and spiritual entity. Mingled as they now were among the conglomerate of all races, nations, and tongues that Nebuchadnezzar had removed from their homes for the purpose of having at hand a mighty work force, a great gang of forced laborers, Israel was merely existing in a dry and weary land. God had even promised her a land for herself, a land flowing with milk and honey; but that period of prosperity was finished, too.

Yet this weary period of exile, the fifty years of defeat of body, mind, and spirit (and of course for those enduring it no one knew how long it would last, perhaps even forever), was that "moment," right within the century when the world's great religions took their rise, when two more world religions were being conceived though not yet born, only conceived in the womb of the chaotic and unregulated life of Babylon. For it is from this moment of seeming annihilation and abject humiliation that both Judaism and Christianity took their rise. Not that these faiths were born in that sixth century B.C., as I have said. Both of them had known a long preparatory period before that time. But it took another seeming "end" in Israel's story, the year A.D. 70, when the Romans wiped Jerusalem off the map, for Talmudic Judaism to be born. In the same way

Christianity came to the birth only a couple of generations earlier, when the death of Jesus, also at the hand of Rome, ended the period that Jewish thinkers had begun to call "the birth pangs of the Messiah."

In a word, then, that which "died" in the year 587 B.C. was the total religious experience of Israel, which she had gained over the significant period of a thousand years; for everything that Israel had come to believe by that date was now laid in the grave in the dust of Babylon. Yet <u>it was out of this transvaluation of all values, human hopes, and human aspirations that there was born the only religion of all the religions of the world that was essentially not a religion at all, but was rather a total revelation of the meaning of life as it was meant for all men, and which was intended to be lived out, not in terms of "religion" as such, but rather in terms of obedience to the mind of God</u>. This obedience was meant to be lived out within a particular relationship that God himself had first created, that of a covenant, created for the purpose of binding one particular people with himself. This new understanding of God in the sixth century was thus not just another philosophy about human existance; nor was it a code of social ethics; nor again just "another road up the mountain with God at the top"; certainly it was not merely another religion to add to the many already existing in the world. In fact, the word "religion" does not even occur in the Old Testament. <u>This new understanding of historical event required a person's total response to what God *had already done* in history, a response of obedience, gratitude, and joy</u>.

CHAPTER 2

Israel's Share in This World Movement

*F*OR AN UNDERSTANDING OF BIBLICAL THEOLOGY ISRAEL'S exile in Babylon, beginning in part from 597 B.C., and then wholly from 587, is the foundation on which all else is built. We ought then to note the voices of some of those who underwent this total collapse of meaning.

Jeremiah saw the collapse coming as he watched the Babylonian empire grow and expand in power and might. Its king was known as "King of kings and Lord of lords." Jeremiah awaited in horror the arrival of Nebuchadnezzar's hordes. He described Babylon in terms of the mythical monster of Babylon's own religious tradition, *Ti'amat*, the power of evil that Israel later personified as Leviathan, or Rahab, or Serpent, or Dragon, the Monster of the Deep, who had devoured Israel in 587 and had crushed her; "he has swallowed me like a monster; he has filled his belly with my delicacies, he has rinsed me out" (Jer. 51:34).

Job represents the typical, thoughtful, God-fearing Israelite who is compelled to ask the question that all suffering people come eventually to shout to the skies, especially when they are dispossessed of home and promised land, the question posed in the one word "Why?" Job's world had collapsed in every respect. He, too, makes use of the thought-forms of his age, and speaks of Sheol and Abaddon, of Leviathan and the Serpent, employing them quite naturally in his struggle to find meaning in the mystery of evil. Can there be any meaning to things when the ordered life of man under God, king, and moral law have come to an end, so that all that is left is the jungle (as we say today), or, as the Israel of Job's day put the same idea, the wilderness from which God

7

had rescued Israel in days of long ago. The wilderness was of course the place where wild beasts roamed, politically and socially speaking on the one hand, and psychologically and personally on the other (Matt. 4:1; Luke 4:1). But Job never suggests that the answer lies in the strength of man to overcome the desert, that is to say, the pains and sorrows of life. God alone must do so.

A number of *Psalms,* obviously written during the Exile, raise the same piercing cry of "Why?" "O God, why dost thou cast us off for ever?" (As I have suggested, the exiles must have thought this was their case, because, of course, they could not see into the future.) "Remember Mount Zion, where thou hast dwelt.... The enemy has destroyed everything in the sanctuary!... They set thy sanctuary on fire; to the ground they desecrated the dwelling place of thy name.... We do not see our signs [religious symbols]; there is no longer any prophet.... How long, O God?" (Ps. 74:1-10).

The five poems in the book of *Lamentations* echo the same cry. These were penned soon after the "end" of Jerusalem had occurred so brutally and finally. "The enemy has stretched out his hands over all her precious things; yea, she has seen the nations invade her sanctuary." "Her people trade their treasures for food." But like both Job and the Psalmist above, the writer lays the cause of the disaster firmly at the door of the Lord. "The Lord has become like an enemy, he has destroyed Israel.... The Lord has brought to an end in Zion appointed feast and Sabbath.... The Lord has scorned his altar.... The Lord determined to lay in ruins the wall of the daughter of Zion." Jeremiah agreed with such sentiments, for, speaking for God, he could say as the Babylonian army drew near, "Nebuchadnezzar my servant...."

Ezekiel was a priest of the Jerusalem Temple. He was carried off to Babylon with the first deportation after the first investment of the city in 597 B.C. There in the far country he was waiting with mounting torment the inevitable fall of Jerusalem, that total annihilation of Israel's political, social, religious, and cultic life which did in fact eventuate a decade later—and his torment was that he waited for *God* to do it. We may use the phrase "the death of Israel" advisedly, for that is how Ezekiel describes it. Moreover, since it was neither a natural death nor a form of suicide, it could be seen only as an act of God comparable with that in which Joshua on God's behalf put the city of Jericho "to the ban," laid it under a *ḥerem*, exterminated it, forfeited its right to exist. For it was not just the ancient city of bricks and mortar that had now been hurled to the ground, that city whose ancient name was *Jeru-shalom;* it was Zion that "died" in that fateful year, Zion being the poetic name not just of Jerusalem but also of "the people of God," that people with whom God had made covenant a thousand years before, saying at that time to his chosen people: "I will be your God, and you will be my people—*and I will never let you go.*" Thus, in the death of the divine promise, one could be tempted to suppose that when the city fell he who had made the promise actually died himself. There was ample evidence for such a terrible, logical conclusion to this terrible question. "The death of God" was a persistent theme in the mythologies of the entire Near East of the day. It is a persistent theme for many a disillusioned soldier in the wars of our day and generation, too. Therefore, if other religions in the world could entertain such a strange concept as they did of old, then so might Israel in her turn, and so might we today.

Yet Israel never even raised such a possibility, basically because she did not believe that she "possessed a religion" at all. The basic significance of Israel's ancient traditions seemed to have been ridiculed by fate with the events of 587, those traditions whose interpretation was wholly different from those entertained by any of the peoples who were her neighbors—Egyptians, Canaanites, Babylonians, Greeks, Etruscans, or later on, Romans, Parthians, Persians, or later still, Hindus, Buddhists, Jains, Confucianists, or even today, Zen Buddhists, Spiritualists, Rosicrucians, Theosophists, Christian Scientists, Baha'is, Moonies, or any other movement.

This conviction was held by one who called himself only a "voice" (Isa. 40:3). It takes a voice to convey a "word," either from God or man. This voice actually lived *in* the wilderness experience of the Exile, at that time when he had learned so much from his predecessor, Ezekiel the priest, and from his own people with whom he shared the significance of Ezekiel's vision. For his people were now merely bare, dry bones scattered over the Euphrates valley (Ezek. 37). The picture seems to portray the idea that the bones had been bulldozed into a series of mass graves (37:13). In face of the existential experience shown in this parable this "voice" was possessed by the overwhelming conviction that Israel's God was "I am the Lord, that is my name; my glory I give to no other" (Isa. 42:8). "I am God, and henceforth I AM" (Isa. 43:13). "I am the Lord, *and there is nothing else*" (Isa. 45:5). His conviction then was that this God alone is the I AM, for as he himself says, there can be no other, such as a concept invented by the mind of man. The I AM is not a philosophical idea, nor is he a system of ethics. Neither is he identifiable with the universe that he himself created. And certainly he is not *me*; I am not part of the "universal Soul"; for apart from the I AM, *there is nothing else.*

Because of this absolute statement we can now begin to glimpse one aspect of the action of God when he annihilated his own people. For, paradoxically, it was only when that people was "dead and buried"—by God!—when they had been rendered *nothing*, that the revelation could take place in a human heart—not in the heart of some grand charismatic figure who then went on to create one of the world's great religions, a Buddha, a Muhammad, a Moon, but in that of a completely anonymous figure (and to be anonymous, to have no name, means to be without any definable personality). The biblical faith, in other words, arose, not by human thought or effort, but from him who alone IS, and who therefore can reveal himself, since he so wills, where there is no means of communication, no life, no thought, no human wisdom to latch onto, even no symbols, as we saw in the statements of Lamentations quoted above. For those to whom the I AM chose to reveal himself were dry bones, lying in their graves, in a land of chaos and of nonbeing.

How then could such a thing as this miracle of revelation, given not to the living but to the dead, have come about at all? This important question does, of course, have an answer. And the answer lies, not in human philosophies or religions, but in history, that aspect of God's creation which, in his own wisdom, he chose to be the vehicle, the "symbol," of his revelation to man.

We seem to be suggesting that the revelation was made only in the mid-period of Israel's history, and not at its beginning. Just as the so-called historical books in the Old Testament do not begin "at the beginning" of the story, but are preceded by a theological prologue, so we in our turn must examine this same "prologue" to receive the guidance we need to understand why God used the "death" of Israel, rather than her birth, to reveal himself to the world. That "prologue" is contained in the first eleven chapters of Genesis.

CHAPTER 3

The Exile from Within

W HEN SHAKESPEARE WROTE HIS DRAMAS IN THE FORM OF
stories in, normally, five-act plays, he did not leave the
finished drama with the last scene of the last act. First of all,
while still working at the story, he turned back to the
beginning and inserted there a Prologue to the whole play. In
it he indicated in what direction the story would proceed.
Then, similarly, he might write an Epilogue and place it at the
conclusion of Act V. By means of this device he tied together
the whole work, thus summarizing what the story had had to
say.

The Bible contains, similarly, a Prologue and an
Epilogue. Neither is meant to be historical narrative. Rather,
each is didactic in intention. The book of Revelation,
professedly a dream, pulls together all the threads of the
divine comedy in symbols drawn from within one or more of
the various acts of the drama that has now been unfolded.
Similarly, having been presented with the historical drama in
its various acts that comprises Scripture, one is glad to have
the following questions answered from outside of the drama
of salvation itself in a Prologue: Where did the drama take
place? Among whom did it take place? Why did it have to take
place at all? How did the divine Author set about solving his
own problem?

Just as Shakespeare probably wrote his Prologue after he
was well into, say, Act III of his play, since only by then was
he quite sure how his story would develop, so too with our
divine comedy. The first chapter of Genesis was penned at a
time when the overwhelming awareness of God's purposes
had come home to those Israelites who were experiencing—

12

existentially—the horror of God's activity among them as they sought to put meaning into the meaninglessness of the Exile. Those chapters of Isaiah that we suggest came from the mind of the unknown, and therefore quite uncharismatic and indefinable human writer, whom we can only name Deutero-Isaiah, namely, chapters 40–55 of that book, without any doubt, as we gather from internal evidence, belong to the end period of the Exile. But a large part of the Old Testament writings also originates during the Exile. For centuries before this, Israel had jealously held firmly to her sacred traditions. From very early times these had been handed down in spoken form, as has been the case in most preliterate societies, so that only later on did they find final expression in the written word. Yet even when they were set down in writing they could hardly have been said to be "final." This is true for several reasons. For example, in those days the Hebrew language made use of consonants only. Thus its speakers, when reading Hebrew aloud (for all people read aloud in those days), had to pronounce each consonant in its relation to the next one by making use of what we would call vowel sounds. But the latter were not written as part of the word. Inevitably, therefore, the written tradition could on occasions be understood in more ways than one. A clear instance of the ease with which a "consonant only" writing system could result in reading the text in different ways is the use that the New Testament Epistle to the Hebrews makes of a verse as it quotes the Old Testament book of Genesis. In the latter, at 47:31, we read: "Then Israel bowed himself upon the head of his bed." But in Hebrews 11:21 we read: "...bowing in worship over the head of his staff." The Hebrew word for "bed" employs the three consonants *m-t-h*, and as such it must be pronounced *mittah*. The word for "staff," on the other hand, also uses the consonants *m-t-h*, but these are to be read as *matteh*.

Then again, it is clear that early Israel made use of more than one tradition. This is understandable when we recall that, after the reign of Solomon, the northern tribes broke away from the rule of the kings in Jerusalem. For the next two centuries, when Judah and Ephraim were at times hardly on speaking terms, it is natural that the early traditions of the people should come to vary. It is surprising, on the other hand, by how little they did vary, and that when they did, the variation was only in inessentials. Thus when "Jerusalem's" memory of the story of Joseph, to which we give the symbol J, came to be laid alongside "Samaria's" memory (or "Ephraim's," and so the symbol E), once the northern kingdom had been overrun and occupied by Sargon the Assyrian king in 722, the two traditions were combined into one tale—including even their disagreements! One tradition tells us that it was Ishmaelites to whom the brothers sold the young Joseph (Gen. 37:27); but another tradition (seen in the next verse) thought it was Midianites who had pulled Joseph up out of the pit. And so the compiler reconciled the two memories in the second part of that verse by including them both. Accuracy is not of course essential for the transmission of Israel's tradition. Some of it in fact is in the form of saga, which represented folk-memory rather than exact historical writing. The whole question of how and when the Exodus from Egypt took place, and how many Israelites were involved in it, is very much an open one. It is what the ancient events lead to that matters. They lead to that historical moment, which cannot be gainsaid, to that factual event in time, when Israel experienced a total loss of all that had preceded in her historical and spiritual story, namely, the fall of Jerusalem that took place in 587 B.C.

There was a third school of writing that was of the utmost importance. We designate it by the symbol P, because it appears to be the work of a succession of priestly scholars. These learned men accepted as valid the two earlier "streams" of tradition, along with the Deuteronomic revision made in the seventh century. Now they added their own immensely valuable material, some of which was as old as J's. Altogether these streams formed the greater part of the Pentateuch, the first five books of Moses, that we have now. The value of P is that it offers a priestly interpretation of the stories already known to the people, much as the Fourth Gospel does to the various strands of material common to the Synoptic Gospels. Leviticus, for example, offers us some very ancient material, but at chapter 16, not only do we find a description of the ritual connected with the Day of Atonement as it had come to be seen in the sixth century, but also a theological interpretation of what it was all about. This interpretation came into being after Deutero-Isaiah wrote his fifty-third chapter, which deals with the Suffering Servant, while it in turn was an interpretation of the factual experience of the Exile. In short, then, we have said all this to show how the revelation we have received from the fact of the Exile is something different from the teaching even of the great prophets. The ancient stories and teachings are not necessarily recorded in the manner the biblical literalist would like to believe. The Old Testament is not an infallible book. What is infallible is the fact of the Exile.

We know that priests of the Jerusalem Temple were undoubtedly among those who were transported to Babylon in 597 and 587 B.C. In addition, the book of Ezra informs us that a large proportion of the returnees to Zion in and after 537 B.C. were in fact priests and temple officials. Many such would have been the first to return home and to have been those most involved in the rebuilding of the Temple. The edifice was completed in 516 and dedicated the following year.

These five years of rebuilding must have been very exciting ones for the priests and Levites. During the Exile their fathers had sat at the feet of Ezekiel and his fellow-priests. Their sons and daughters now heard the heartwarming voice of Deutero-Isaiah (and many people think he remained invisible to the exiles, only sending forth his "chapters" in the form of broadsheets for distribution to the small worshipping groups on the housetops on Sabbath days), as he proclaimed the coming of God's "Messiah," Cyrus, king of the Persians (Isa. 45:1). Israel's God, he wrote, had raised up this prince to "set the prisoners free." Deutero-Isaiah now reinterpreted the whole story of God's ways with Israel right from the days of Abraham, in such a manner that this "strange" revelation was evidently warmly received, especially by members of the priestly schools. What they did, it seems, was to incorporate much of what he said into Israel's sacred literature, and to adapt it for use in the liturgy that was to be adopted once the Temple should be complete again. This new liturgy thus helped the ordinary man to "act out" the meaning of God's ways with Israel. It allowed him to participate in the ritual himself, so that the meaning of it all came alive for him in a personal way.

And so we must now return to the first chapter of Genesis. The priestly school had prepared this chapter for liturgical use, under the influence of the theological interpretation of the historical events that the exiles had lived through, and which had been expressed by the great prophets who had lived in the Exile themselves. It was now seen to be so important for the whole revelation of God to man that it was set down as the prime Introduction, in the form of "Chapter 1," to the whole of the Pentateuch, the five Scrolls, the first five books of the Bible.

CHAPTER 4

Israel's Creating God

*T*HE RENDERING OF THE FIRST VERSE OF GENESIS IN THE
King James Version ("In the beginning God created...")
did the cause of biblical theology a great disservice. This
rendering suggests that we have before us a finite verb,
meaning "he created." Fortunately, none of the recent
English versions repeats this error. One result of this
rendering of the verse, once England had made itself at home
with the Authorized Version, was the rise, within the Church
of England particularly, of the view of God in his relationship
to the world that we call Deism. The King James Version
seems to suggest that at the beginning God created the
universe in much the same way as a watchmaker would fit
together the pieces needed to build a watch or a clock. Then
he wound it up, went away, and left it to run on its own
resources. Since God had wound up the universe similarly, he
could then become an absentee divinity. He had now left the
universe to tick away on its own momentum, to move along
without his help, even to "evolve," if you like the word, as it
was even then doing in eighteenth-century England. The
only correct translation of the verse is one that reveals that we
are not dealing with the issue of the creation of the cosmos at
all.

Exegeting the first three verses of Genesis strictly on the
basis of the grammar of the language, we find that all three
verses form only one sentence. A true sentence exists only
when it contains a finite verb. The only finite verb we have in
these three sentences as they are found in the Authorized
Version is the word "said." In the English we meet it only at
verse 3. So we must examine what this fact entails.

It would seem that, once the Hebrew text of Genesis had been translated into the Greek version known as the Septuagint somewhere around 250 B.C., the Hebrew consonants began to be repronounced to fit the Greek meaning of the words that had emerged. The translation was made in Alexandria, Egypt, at that period very much part of the world of Hellenic culture. We shall have more to say later on this interesting issue of the influence of a translator's cultural heritage on his work. The LXX reads: "In the beginning God made...," not "created," a choice of term evidently influenced by Greek philosophical thinking. But the original text of the sixth century B.C. had read: "In the beginning of God's creating...," or, in better English, "When God began to create...," the form we find in a footnote to the RSV. From this rendering, accordingly, we understand that God has never given up creating, but always continues to do so. That theological assertion can in no sense be defined as Deism.

Both the NEB and the TEV make it clear that verse 2 continues as a second subordinate clause that does not have a finite verb. It reads, "And when the earth was without form and void." These last English nouns represent two Hebrew words, *tohu* and *bohu.* The latter occurs only once again, in a quotation of this first verse of Genesis. So we recognize that it is only an alliterative form, used to emphasize what is a strange term. The noun *tohu* is strange, for it is not a Hebrew word at all.

The Hebrews took it over from the Babylonians—not from the generation they met when in exile in the 500's, but from the civilization that the patriarchs had known a whole millennium before. Whatever this word means, its being there in the text indicates that God did not create *ex nihilo,* as Greek thought continually supposed. Nowhere in the Old Testament is it even suggested that the earth was created out of nothing. This means that any modern scientific theory on the origin of the universe, whether it be the "Big Bang" theory or any other, must be argued strictly from its own premises, and must not look to the Bible for support. Genesis 1–11 is a theological statement in picture language handling the revelation of the nature and purpose of God. It is not a scientific document, and could not have been expected to be. Only in the Apocrypha do we have mention of *creatio ex nihilo*. But the Apocrypha was rejected as Holy Scripture in the early Christian centuries by both Synagogue and Church. One reason for doing so is that, like certain parts of the LXX, it displays at times the intrusion of Greek philosophical thinking into the unique theology of the Old Testament.

In the days of the patriarchs (2000 B.C.[?] to 1500 B.C.[?]) the region of Mesopotamia had come to believe that in the beginning the god Marduk had vanquished and slain the goddess *Ti'amat,* cutting her into two pieces in "devilish" delight. This goddess was the representation of the waters of chaos ("the waters under the earth") that are mentioned in Exodus 20:4. Her other half comprised the waters above the sky. She personalized these chaotic waters that were there in the beginning, showing herself in the form of the Dragon or as Leviathan.

Israel did not accept such myths as the answer to the questions all men feel bound to ask about the origin of the world. This was because (a point we shall amplify later) Israel believed that there could only be one reality, namely, God. Deutero-Isaiah makes this point in the words: "I am the Lord, and there is nothing else." This means that all that we regard as "creation" has been brought into being by God in order to fulfill his purposes, so that they can also disappear should God but "withhold his breath." But Israel made use of the form of the Mesopotamian myth as a vehicle of thought, and so of revelation, just as Jesus used the form of the parable to teach the truth about God.

So, taking the name of the Babylonian goddess of chaos, and leaving off the feminine suffix *-at* to show their disbelief in myth, and introducing into the word an internal aspirate as a Cockney can do in English, the priestly school produced in Hebrew the word *tehom,* the word that is translated by the English word "deep" in Genesis 1:2.

The deep, the abyss, although it is now a theological concept and no longer myth, must, however, be described for the sake of our human understanding in language belonging to the world we know. "Darkness was upon the face of the deep" (RSV), "...over the face of the abyss" (NEB), "the raging ocean that covered everything" (TEV). So now we can *see* the meaning of the word *tohu*, since we have been given a picture of it. It is chaos, negation, nonbeing, presented to the human imagination as a hurricane whose colossal waves, in the horror associated with total darkness, could smash in pieces beyond hope any frail craft in which poor humanity might dare to put to sea. In other words, *tehom* was the epitome of *de*struction itself.

However, actually moving over those same waters of the abyss, the Spirit of God is present in a *con*structive capacity. We must now note the meaning of two more words. First, the word rendered here by "was moving" occurs only once more in the Old Testament. Second, the word "spirit" may equally well be rendered "wind." And of course it is wind to which it refers, if we stay merely at the level of the structure of the "myth." But just as at John 3, in Jesus' discussion with Nicodemus, the word for the physical "wind" actually conveys the concept of the spirit of God, so too in Genesis 1:2. Then we note that "spirit" is a feminine noun. Is it that the female is the creative partner in human generation? Certainly here it is "she" who is the agent of the creation of the new life that emerges, could we say, from the chaotic amniotic fluid in the womb of time. The only other positive usage of the verb employed here is that which describes the shuffling action of a mother eagle as she spreads her wings over her clutch of eggs to produce life from these seemingly inert objects. This second time that the verb occurs is in that highly *theological* poem, the Song of Moses (Deut. 32:11).

The creativity of God is finally expressed absolutely by means of the first finite verb of our passage, as we have noted. In verse 3 of the English version we have the words, "And God *said,* 'Let there be light'—and there was light." And so Light *became,* not out of nothing, but over against chaos, nonbeing, unreality, negation, all of which concepts are pictured under the term Darkness. Not *out of* chaos, we note, for Light came forth from the heart and mind of God, and then issued through his lips. Coming forth over against chaos, it did so in spite of chaos. Yet the Light is not mentioned first. Chaos seems to have been there before God's creative activity could begin to be operative; for creation is not creation out of nothing; it is creation out of tension with chaos.

Thereupon, at Genesis 1:4 God equates Light with what is good, and in this way he separates the Good from—what? not from evil. He separates it from Darkness. Darkness is not of course evil in itself. Rather it is that which permits chaos to exist out of sight. God now even goes so far as to *name* chaos, thereby giving it identity and reality in his own mind and for his own purpose, in the same manner as he gives a name to Light. Throughout the rest of the Scriptures this figurative language continues to regard Light and Darkness as identities to be reckoned with. "God is Light, and in him is no darkness at all" (1 John 1:5). "The Lord is my light and my salvation" (Ps. 27:1). "Let us walk in the light of the Lord" (Isa. 2:5). Again, "I am the light of the world" leads to its astonishing parallel, "You are the light of the world" (John 8:12; Matt. 5:14). "It is the Lord who said, 'Let light shine out of darkness' who has shone in our hearts to give the light of the knowledge of the glory of God in the face of Christ" (2 Cor. 4:6).

This reality, then, Deutero-Isaiah expresses with sublime simplicity, immediately after the divine statement: "I am the Lord, and there is nothing else":

> "*I shape* [*handle*] *light but create darkness,*
> *I form* shalom [*integration, wholeness, perfection*]
>   *but create evil*" (Isa. 45:7).

God does not need to create either light or *shalom*. These are of his very nature, and they issue out of his mouth. But he has to create evil since it is the woof of the cosmos, of space and time, even of human life, for these are all rooted in chaos and thus represented under the figure of darkness. What God has created, therefore, he has the power to destroy. But so long as darkness is *there*, permitted by his will to exist, he makes use of it to his own glory. His continuing creative activity thus takes full account of the existence of evil. He uses evil as his servant. Evidently God must need evil to attain the good. For good is not a mere abstraction. It is not what the three monkeys of the East would have us understand: "Hear no evil, see no evil, speak no evil." The biblical "good" is not the opposite of negation. Negation is merely *tohu*. The biblical good is the overcoming of *tohu*, it is the creation of what is wholly new *out of* the chaos, the realm of pain, sorrow, earthquakes, famines, and—most important of all—the sin and rebellion that is characteristic of the human mind and heart.

During the Exile our priestly authors came to discover in an absolute sense three realities about the nature of God. These are expressed in the three verses we have now sought to understand.

(1) God creates. The verb used here, *bara'*, has only God as its subject, never man, except when man acts "under God" and at his command (Josh. 17:15,18). In earlier days, before critical biblical studies were attempted, scholars supposed that its use with God alone as the "actor" meant that God alone can create out of nothing. But the verbal form that we actually find used shows that God never ceases to create, and so to recreate. In recreating, moreover, he does not create out of nothing, but always in the presence of "chaos." God does so by actually employing chaos as the necessary instrument to gain his ends. The active participle of the verb *bara'*, showing God's continuing action, is to be found some 16 times in the pages of Deutero-Isaiah. The latter exemplifies what Genesis says, that God continues to use chaos as the instrument of his purpose.

Genesis has substituted for the myth that was part of ancient thinking a theological usage, all the while retaining the picture language of that myth. The "deep" is still "down below" in Israel's thinking. There it is, we have noted, still down below when it occurs as an element in the Second Commandment. In the same way it is present today in the "depths" of the human subconscious, as every psychologist affirms. The Psalmist had the perspicacity to put the two ideas together when he wrote:

Thou didst knit me together in my mother's womb....
    My frame was not hidden from thee,
When I was being made in secret,
    intricately wrought in the depths of the earth (Ps. 139:15).

Chaos is always with us. Jesus took this for granted when he declared: "Do not worry about tomorrow; it will have enough worries of its own. There is no need to add to the troubles each day brings" (Matt. 6:34 TEV).

(2) God creates through his Spirit. The Spirit is not something other than God. The Spirit *is* God, for it is the Spirit *of* God that creates order where there is chaos, life over against negation. The Spirit does so, not by identifying itself with chaos, but by creative "movement" over the surface of *tehom*. As Creator, God is Actor, Mover; as Spirit, he is still Actor, Mover. In neither case is he mere "being" or "essence." God's Spirit never identifies itself with chaos because chaos is part of creation and is thus of a temporary nature. The Spirit moves *over the face of* chaos only. Chaos is not *of* the nature of God, only light is.

Deutero-Isaiah, then, had experienced the nature of *tohu* in the Exile. He had come to realize the meaning of the divine declaration: "I did not say to the offspring of Jacob, 'Seek me in chaos.' I the Lord speak Reality" (Isa. 45:19). Chaos is not reality; only the light that God *spoke,* said, is reality. These sentences therefore preserve a fundamental revelation that must be taken into account when we attempt to see the relationship of the I AM of Deutero-Isaiah to the theologies of the religions of man.

(3) God creates through his Word. To use an illustration from human experience: we recognize that the creative act that results in the building of a bridge has its source in the personality of one man. Yet this one man spends many years in study—reading, thinking, and planning—before he takes the first step in building. As he plans he becomes aware in his "heart" (the expression the Bible uses for our word "brain") of what he proposes to do. Next he gathers his work force. Only then does he *reveal* the plan that was his in the beginning, which was the creation of his heart and mind. "This is what I want you to do. Go now and build it." The word goes forth in accordance with the laws of mechanics, just as light goes forth according to the laws of physics. In the end it accomplishes the task that was first conceived in the mind of the actor. Thus the bridge eventually becomes a *thing*—in fact, a new

creation. The new bridge is not a physical projection of the pesonality of the engineer, in the manner that the Eastern religions think of God's creative activity. Rather the bridge is an empirical projection of the purpose and plan of the engineer that undoubtedly proceeded from the "heart" of him who thought it up.

When God *said,* "Let there be light," the light proceeded from the heart of God's being. It was never independent of God, any more than the Spirit was. For it was the Light *of God,* just as the Spirit was the Spirit *of God.* But the Light became the empirical projection, not of the essence of God, but of the will and purpose of him who sent it forth out of his mouth to let it crystallize in terms of space and time (Isa. 55:8-11).

Thus even when God proceeds to create, through his Word, he remains God, he remains the wholly Other, the great I AM, and never allows himself to become identifiable with his creation. And so we read next: "And God *said,* 'Let there be a firmament....' " "And God *said,* 'Let the waters be gathered together....' " "And God *said,* 'Let the earth bring forth....' " And such is true even of the crown of creation: "And God *said,* 'Let us make man in our image....' " Man here is not a spark of the divine, united in some way with the essence of God. Creation cannot be conceived in pantheistic terms. The concept of the "Word" safeguards the biblical revelation from being equated with the ideas one finds in India. God cannot be identified with the universe, even with that part of his universe that is his creature man. "Lift this stone and you will find God." Some such utterance was attributed to Jesus in an apocryphal fragment of papyrus found in Egypt. No wonder it has always been considered apocryphal! As Deutero-Isaiah declares: "I am the Lord, and there is nothing else" (Isa. 45:5); or, rather than name this man thus, we should say that these words came, not from Deutero-Isaiah, but from a "voice" that claimed nothing for itself. Yet that voice was heard at the very period when the charismatic, and therefore ego-centered, figure of Buddha was born, and when Hinduism was reconstructing itself in terms of pantheism and philosophical dualism.

It is such a God as this, then, who is the God of the New Testament because he is the God of the Old Testament, and therefore the God of the Christian Faith.

CHAPTER 5

I AM: This Is My Name

WE MUST NOW TRY TO SEE WHAT UNDERSTANDING OF GOD there was in the long period between Genesis 12 (the first "historical" chapter in the Old Testament) and the period of the Exile. Material like the Song of Moses in Deuteronomy 32 can give us a good answer, in that it is one of the earliest pieces of theological writing the world possesses. As we study it we notice that it was one of Deutero-Isaiah's basic texts. Clearly passed on from generation to generation by word of mouth, and expressed in vivid poetry, the Song found written form, most scholars agree, perhaps a century before the reign of King David. The writer begins by inviting the universe to listen as he "proclaims the name of the Lord." Since in ancient Israel the name was the title and description of its owner, what follows interests us immensely. For God's "essence" is described in terms, not of his being, but of his work. His work is his activities in history that reveal his will and his purpose *in this world,* as he utters his will through his Word. This Word of God "descends" on creation and renews it, just as the rain descends on and renews the soil. His work is seen in the form of actions. Yet God cannot do evil in any form at all. He performs only actions of creative love and of "right."

For these last two terms we await Deutero-Isaiah's interpretation. Instead of *doing* evil, God *creates* good with the cooperation of evil, or, as Genesis 1 puts it, by means of chaos. "See now that I, even I, AM; there is no god beside me" (Isa. 45:5), or, as we might say today, "I have only one name." "I work, and who can hinder it?" (Isa. 43:13). "I kill and I make alive; I wound and I heal: and there is none that can deliver out of my hand" (or, to use today's terminology:

"There is no escape from *this* form of divine activity"—Deut. 32:39).

The reader will remember that in Chapter 2 we translated the words of Isaiah 43:13, not, as in the RSV and NEB, by "I am He" (the TEV omits the "name" altogether), but by I AM. He will now notice that the Hebrew words that we read in Isaiah 43 are those which we find here at Deuteronomy 32:39, so that we now give them the same translation. We do so because the Hebrew language possesses no verb "to be," and so cannot say "I am." If the idea of "being" really needs to be expressed, it can be done by means of two pronouns, thus "I–he," as in Deutero-Isaiah's words. To translate these two pronouns literally makes no sense in English. What Hebrew does is to ask the pronoun "he" to act in place of the copula "am." So in both Deuteronomy 32 and Isaiah 43 we correctly translate by using the words "I AM." And the reason why, in the present context, we write "am" in capital letters is that the English translations of Exodus 3:14 express the Hebrew of that passage in just such a vivid manner.

We have also noted earlier that the Old Testament contains ancient traditions of Israel's early days, or, to be more correct, traditions handed down over the years about *the activity of God in Israel's story,* and that these found final form around the days of King Solomon or soon after. One of these is the story we find in Exodus 3.

Israel is now in Egypt. The people are experiencing the hell of mere existence, hardly life at all, the misery of forced labor imposed on a captive people. They had to work seven days a week, in the fierce heat that beats off the "wilderness" sand of Egypt, all under the hand of cruel taskmasters. Throughout the centuries Israelite thinkers used two illustrations to picture the *tehom* God used when he created both nature and man. One was the hurricane at sea in the blackness of midnight; this we have already noted. The other was that fearful place, the wilderness, the habitation of wild beasts and evil spirits, the place of hunger, thirst, and the dehydration of the human spirit as well as of the human body. Israel in Egypt, then, was tasting *tehom.*

Moses, too, in misery of spirit, was tasting *tehom.* He was tending sheep at the "back side" of the wilderness, *behind* it (today we speak of a place as being "behind God's back"), and so came to Horeb. That very name means "desolation." Yet that same desolate place was the mountain *of God*, the place where God *sur*-mounted *tehom*. We recall the significance of the second verse of Genesis for this. Now we discover an application of the third verse. For it was *there* that "the angel of the Lord" met with Moses. We read too much into the word "angel" if we picture it as many do today. For we carry in our mind images of winged beings framed in stained glass windows. The word "angel" means simply "one sent." We have no description, therefore, of this messenger here. The emphasis is on God's sending, not on what the messenger looked like. He merely emerges from the flames of fire, which again mark the dancing heat of the desert.

In the following encounter God remains God, and Moses the man remains the creature. Once again, however, it is the Word of God that leaps across the chasm that lies between them. In as many words God *said* to Moses, "Be aware that you are creature and that I am God"; in fact, "Not only your God, I am also the God of your ancestors all down the ages." God is faithful, as Deuteronomy 32:4 also claims; he does not change.

Through his Word God then reveals to Moses that he is the God who brings forth good by means of chaos, who brings light out of darkness; and so he calls on Moses to *act in the same way*. Moses is to act for the God who creates, who recreates in face of the reality of chaos, by bringing forth "my people" out of the reality of the cruel civilization of Egypt. The sign of this newness of life will be that they will worship the Creator-Redeemer on that same mountain. God does not accept the worship of his creatures unless they address to him the love and praise that he has already given to them.

But Moses prevaricates. "I am only a creature; I am not God," he says. At which point he hears the Word: "[I declare] that I AM with you." The sentence begins with the particle *ki*, which in a statement such as this usually means "that." Thus it implies a solemn oath preceding the word "that." So we must insert some form of declaratory statement, promise, or even oath. Then the English "I will be" that follows *ki* is identical with the I AM at verse 14, printed in capitals, that Moses goes on to hear. Of course there are no capitals in the Hebrew original. Nor does the Hebrew language employ tenses, as English does. The Hebrew *'ehyeh*, "I will be," at verse 12 is the same word as that which is rendered "I am" at verse 14. In verses 13-15 we listen to God himself (in the form that the ancient tradition reports it) explaining just what "I will be with you" means, and how, being the faithful God that he is, he will never go back on his word. So now we must examine this usage carefully, remembering that the book of Exodus was not written in English.

Moses asks God to pinpoint for him his identity (his "name"). The answer comes, "*'ehyeh 'asher 'ehyeh*," translated basically "I am who I am." But this translation, while partly correct, does not exhaust the meaning of the "name." We have mentioned before that the translators of the Hebrew Bible, living as they did in the Hellenized city of Alexandria, sometimes showed their unexamined prejudice for the philosophical approach to religion that characterized Greek culture—but that is just what some biblical scholars do today, sometimes blissfully unaware of their neo-Platonist ideology. The LXX, then, translates this Hebrew "name" of God by *ego eimi ho ōn*. These words we might translate, approximately, by "I am the existent One." By A.D. 400 the Vulgate had, in its turn, translated this Greek rendering by the Latin *ego sum qui sum*. And so by turning a Hebraic expression into a Latinized name for God we get the Authorized Version rendering I AM WHO I AM.

But such a translation introduces us to a God who, as Pascal put it, is not the God of the Bible but the God of the philosophers, and, we might add, the God of the Hindu mystics as well. The verbal form *'ehyeh* does not simply mean "I am." There is a plus to it that scholars like Jerome, who translated the Bible into the Vulgate (an unwitting product of his Greco-Roman civilization), did not understand. While he went to the trouble of studying Hebrew before he made his important translation into the "common tongue" of the medieval Church, he did not sit at the feet of any Jewish rabbi and ask him what the Hebrew verb *hayah*, as it is used in Scripture, really means in relation to the God whom we meet in the first chapter of Genesis. The verb *hayah* does not describe mere static being; so it is not merely "is." Within this verb there are both movement and vitality. "And it came to pass," a clause that uses this verb, is very common throughout the Old Testament; even our English rendering can show this sense of movement. "The word of the Lord that *came* to Hosea..." is how that book begins. Movement, always movement, nothing static; so that when this verb of "being" occurs it brings with it a vision of proceeding in a particular direction. Thus the English word "become" must be added to the idea of "being" when we meet this verb *hayah*. So we now try to express this idea in God's address to Moses: "I declare that I will become *with* you." '*Ehyeh* indeed means I AM, but it means more. For included in its usage is a totally new and different understanding of the divine name now being expressed in terms of movement, in which we read, "I AM has *sent* me to you."

The whole book of Exodus was finally edited by the priestly school during the Babylonian Exile. "P," as we call him (or them), therefore adds his own interpretation to what he has found in the ancient tradition of "J." Exodus 6:2 looks like a repetition of what we have already read at chapter 3. There, at verse 15, the narrative had continued, "Say this to the people of Israel, 'The Lord...has sent me to you.' "In Hebrew the word we translate as LORD made use of the consonants of our verb *hayah* as they appear in a transitive, or creative, form. P now comments in chapter 6:2 on the usage found in chapter 3. The reading there is composed of two words, '*ani* (meaning "I"), and then *y-h-w-h*. Again there is no word for "am," as in Deutero-Isaiah. The two words thus mean "I, Yahweh." Yet we are presented with the problem of how the four consonants that now express the "name" of God are to be pronounced. This has been a matter of conjecture all through the centuries. Not wishing even to utter the sacred name, the ancient Jew put the vowels used in the quite different word "Lord" onto the bare consonants that we have in Exodus 6:2, and then pronounced the name as LORD, as we ourselves do in English. But however we pronounce the "Sacred Tetragrammaton," P believed that its content must be that which we have had revealed to us already in Genesis 1:1-3. The LORD's name, that is to say, his very nature, his essence, is not to be understood as mere "being," for it is clearly to be seen as creative activity as well. But P goes further still. God's activity, he declares, will focus only on a certain segment of humanity he has created. In addressing Moses as "thee" (singular), God had been addressing the head of the body, the top of the triangle, the representative of the whole people of God. We see this to be true, without pursuing the argument further at this point, as we watch the story unfold in the pages of the Old Testament.

Yet we are left with two different Hebrew expressions for I AM. We have noted that P used a particular form of this verb to give us the name Yahweh. The other is the form *'ani hou'* ("I am He") with which we began, and which is used by Deutero-Isaiah. Yet P, at Exodus 6:2, has already begun to identify the two forms when he reports that God said *"'ani Yahweh"* ("I am Yahweh"). In fact we can see how Deutero-Isaiah, who surely mixed with this active priestly group in Babylon, pours into his "name" for God, which is *'ani hou'*, this content which we now expect to find, since "with you" had long been part of the divine name. A study even of one of his chapters, namely, chapter 43, is sufficient to make this plain.

CHAPTER 6

I AM with You

*I*SAIAH 43 BEGINS, AS WE CAN SEE, WITH THE VERB *BARA'*,
a verb that we render by the English "create," and which
we found in the first verse of Genesis. Moreover, it is
significant that throughout the 16 chapters of Deutero-Isaiah
this verb occurs consistently in the form of the active
participle. This is the grammatical form required by Hebrew
to express, not once-for-all-ness, but continuing activity. God
is he who keeps on creating, or, as the case may be, on
recreating; and, in light of what we have already discovered
about the usage of *bara'* in Genesis 1:1-3, it must mean
constant recreating out of, or by means of, or with the help of,
what may be an evil situation.

So we read at Isaiah 43:1: "But now thus says the Lord, he
who continues to create you, O Jacob." This active participle
occurs in contrast with the finite verb of the next verse, where
we read: "Fear not, for *I have redeemed* you," a once-for-all
expression to which we shall return later. Redemption is in
reality an aspect of recreation. "You are mine," continues the
passage; "When you pass through the waters I–*with* you"—
exactly as God had said to Moses. "When you walk through
fire"—perhaps an echo of the Burning Bush episode—"you
will not be burned." "[I declare] that *'ani Yahweh,* your God"
(v. 3), "the Holy One of Israel, your Savior."

At this point we may draw an important inference from
the divine statement "I will become with you" that Deutero-
Isaiah had inherited from the J document of the Pentateuch. It
is that God will continue to reveal himself in and through
personal relationships with his chosen "you." This reality is
evident throughout the entire biblical revelation. Moreover,

the inference carries the corollary that the revelation of God's redemptive love that a person "comes" to discover and accept, even as the Word "comes" to Hosea, is meant to be passed on to others once again through personal relationships. This reality is now summed up in the last phrase of verse 3, "the Holy One *of Israel*." This is a title for Yahweh that was invented by Isaiah of Jerusalem, and which is of frequent use in the earlier chapters of the book of Isaiah. The framework of this "revelation through personal relationships," then, is well described under the very biblical idea of "covenant."

There is controversy about where Israel discovered the idea of the covenant, and there is discussion on just what the word meant to the pagan kings and nations of the days of Moses and Joshua when Israel adopted both the term and the idea behind it. Suffice it to say that in the description given us in Exodus 19 of the giving of the Covenant to Israel, in the promise "I will become with you" the content of the word "you" has been extended from the reference merely to the figurehead at the top of the triangle to the whole people of Israel. As a result of centuries of thought and speculation on what Israel, with Moses as intermediary, had discovered about God on Mount Sinai, by the time of the Exile in Babylon the people had certainly come to *know* that they belonged in a special relationship to Yahweh; for countless events and incidents in their history, beginning with their escape from Egypt, had gone to prove that it was so. And yet, now that Jerusalem was in ruins, as all Israel also *knew*, it seemed that the covenant relationship had been an illusion all along. In the same way, when we compare the faith of Israel with the other religions that were born in the spacious sixth century B.C., we find that the very idea of the biblical covenant relationship is regarded as a mere illusion by those who espouse a selfish search for salvation, or by those who espouse no religion at all. The present-day wave of secularism that has swept over the West has left millions who were formerly Christians like empty husks. Since nature abhors a vacuum, what we now discover is another form of selfish, individualistic search for salvation. Young people sometimes seek "salvation" in enticing sects that batten on this emptiness of the human spirit, or rush to the feet of a guru. The latter may be an Indian ascetic in the mountains of India, or he may even be the Jesus of the Gospels, once he has been separated from his setting in the biblical covenant. For without the Covenant, the Christian faith loses both its meaning and its challenge to the peoples of the modern world.

In Exodus 19:5-6 we are given the terms of the Covenant. In the first place, we meet here that particularism which is the mark of the nature of the God who is I AM, and which is anathema to the other gods and philosophies of the world. It is found in the phrase, "You are my own possession among all peoples." God is, of course, possessor of all the earth; all people and nations are his. Yet this one people is now his "special" choice. This people is special, however, not because it is nicer, or better educated, or more powerful, or rejoices in owning more wise men or religiously minded persons than other nations (Deut. 7:6ff.). God enters into personal relationships with Israel, not in order that Israel might be removed out of the toils and tribulations of life to live in a heavenly fellowship with the giver of the Covenant. It is tragic that this kind of thinking is what some Christians today suppose is the meaning of salvation. Rather, and arising from God's special relationship to Israel, Israel is to respond to God's gracious gift in two ways.

First, as a corporate body she is to be a kingdom (under God the King) of priests. Priests perform the liturgy and teach and preach, not in an empty shrine, but in the presence of, and for the good of, others. Israel, then, as her share in the Covenant, is to enter into creative personal relationships with all the nations of the earth that belong to God, and in this way to mediate to all men the fellowship God has already bestowed on her in his peculiar particularistic way. What she has to do is to pass on this fellowship to all people. As Deutero-Isaiah puts it: "I am making you into a light to the nations [cf. Gen. 1:3], that my salvation may 'become' to the end of the earth." God's covenantal particularism is thus not based on favoritism, but bestowed for a task, for "movement" toward the achievement of God's creative and purposeful ends. Israel, then, is elected, not to be saved, but to serve.

Second, Israel is to be a holy nation. She cannot be the instrument of God's holy purpose ("for I am holy, says the Lord") unless she herself is holy first. This she manifestly cannot be of her own strength of mind and purpose.

The book of Leviticus, while containing material going back to Moses, was also edited by P after the fall of Jerusalem, that is to say, after Israel had had demonstrated before her stubborn eyes that she had never been a holy people at any time. Yet the whole theme of Leviticus is that Israel is in fact a holy people, and that she is so simply because God has declared her to be holy. The religious prescriptions in the book and the moral law that is included in it, especially the so-called Holiness Code (chaps. 17–26), are not demands laid on Israel that she must follow in order to become holy. That would be a Buddhist way of thinking. Israel *is* holy, already. The demands laid on her are for quite another purpose; she is to follow the laws that God has given her in order that she might remain holy, and not allow herself to fall out of the covenantal relationship that God in his grace had bestowed on her. God has imputed holiness to her, by grace alone. Thus she may remain holy by accepting the personal fellowship of her holy God, the God who had said to Moses: "I will become with you."

So we return to Isaiah 43:3. There the I AM is referred to as "the Holy One of Israel." In Hebrew this is only two words—one about God, and one about man. Yet they were actually written together as one, in what we call the construct relationship. In this way they exhibit an unbelievable paradox, namely, "The-Holy-One-of-Israel." The wholly other, the unreachable and unsearchable "I AM, and apart from me there is nothing else," is here coupled with sinful Israel. What insight these greatest of all thinkers of the ancient world—Isaiah and his tradition—possessed! It goes far beyond anything that the Socrates-Plato school was ever able to reach when they flourished two centuries later. But then, we should not compare the two schools. The prophets of Israel possessed the unspeakable advantage of already being *in* the Covenant that I AM had granted to his people Israel. Accordingly, it was by grace alone that they were able to claim

possession of the holiness of God, for the grace in which they
knew they stood was already God's gift!

That awareness, then, leads to the next "name" for God,
that of Savior. Deutero-Isaiah has two emphases here. First,
in verse 1, we have God saying, "Don't be afraid, for [*ki*, or "I
declare that"] I have redeemed you." Here the verb used is
that found in the book of Ruth. There we read that the
next-of-kin is obliged to act for any member of the family who
becomes orphaned; he must lift him out of the chaotic life of
those outside the Covenant and bring him into the *shalom*,
peace, wholeness, even "wholesome" way of life that God,
through Moses, had bestowed on Israel. This rule applied
within Israel itself as the family of God. But the author of
Ruth deliberately asks us to realize that the ancestress of
Israel's great king David, king by God's choice, had been
redeemed *out of* chaos *into* the joy and fellowship of Israel's
life with God (Ruth 3:12-13; 4:1-17). Just as "all the people
who were at the gate, and the elders, said, 'We are witnesses' "
(Ruth 4:11), so Deutero-Isaiah writes, " 'You are my witnesses,' says the Lord" (Isa. 43:10), to the possibilities of this very
act.

Second, at 43:3 "Savior" is the active participle of the
verb *yasha*', meaning "to bring into a wide open space." By
using a participle, as in the case of *bara*', Deutero-Isaiah
means that God's saving action goes on and on. God keeps on
recreating, always bringing new things out of the old, and so
here constantly bringing Israel back out of the cramping,
narrowing state of self-love and narrow-mindedness she kept
relapsing into, and leading her into a broad, expansive state
such as an army discovered (for this was probably the original
meaning of the verb *yasha*') when it escaped from the enemy
that was hemming it in and reached the flat, open plain. There
they could lie down in safety, for the watchman could see for
miles if any danger threatened.

Isaiah 43:4 continues: "For you are precious in my eyes"
(the "my own possession among all peoples" of Exod. 19:6),
"and honored"—what kind of God is this to say that of this
scattering of hopeless, displaced persons among Babylon's
millions? — "and I love you." Here we reach the climax of it

all. Deuteronomy 7:8 had said that God had chosen Israel "because the Lord loves you." The "I AM with you" (v. 5) is in fact present with Israel in this creative manner—because he loves her. He loves her as a Bridegroom loves his Bride, whom he has selected from all the possible contestants for this honor, from among the rich, the educated, the philosophically minded, or the punctiliously religious peoples of the earth. But Israel herself had not contended for this honor. God's choice of her as his Bride came to her actually as Good News, as Gospel, as a glorious and exciting surprise. "I shall bring [home to Zion] everyone who is called by my name [who has received my surname, my family name, through marriage], whom I created [*bara'*] for my glory" (43:7). And all this is to happen that you may become existentially aware of me, by putting your whole trust in me, and thus recognizing objectively that I AM (my translation of v. 10b).

This *with-ness* of I AM to his specially selected people is expressed in a number of figures. Deutero-Isaiah's figure of marriage, which he took over from Hosea and Ezekiel, is only one such. Exodus 4:22 declares, "Thus says the Lord, 'Israel is my first-born son,' and I say to you, 'Let my son go that he may serve me.'" This phrase thus leads to the next figure, that of "servant"(Isa. 43:10), which appears at the heart of the preaching of this anonymous "voice" (Isa. 40:3, 6), this contemporary of Zoroaster, Buddha, and Confucius, who lived at the period of the formation of the great Hindu epics. So we read, "You, Israel, my servant"(Isa. 41:8); "You are my servant, I have chosen you" (41:9). In 42:1-9 God describes his servant in some detail. There Israel is God's loved one, with whom God has united himself by his Spirit. The Spirit has now taken the place of Israel's ego, which has now (ideally speaking, and always to be understood in terms of grace) been entirely emptied out. Consequently Israel *now does what God does*, which is to bring the knowledge of God's loving plan to all people. God and Israel therefore work hand in hand (fancy a master humbly taking his slave's hand!), so that *together* Israel's covenant task—to bring light to the nations—may be accomplished. It is God who effects all this, of course, but the Israel that dwells in space and time is God's hands and feet and mouth in the world. Wholly unworthy of this honor as Israel is, God selects her and her alone, refusing to give his glory (the outer radiance of his presence) to any other.

After outlining at 49:1-13 how God has prepared his servant over the centuries for the task ahead, that of bringing both those Israelites in the "prison house" of Babylon and all people everywhere, by means of this unique covenant relationship, out of darkness into God's marvellous light, at long last, at 50:4-11, the servant speaks. Israel confesses the frailty of her frame; she must rely totally on the divine partner in the covenant. The passage Isaiah 52:13–53:12 approaches the task of the servant, in covenant, from still another angle. In it the more-than-human weakness of the servant is sketched in memorable language, a weakness (such as Israel suffered in Babylon) that was marked by disease, ill-treatment, imprisonment, and finally by being cut off from the land of the living. But the great *I AM with you*, who had placed his Spirit in Israel, was now actually suffering himself, in the flesh of Israel, all that the servant had to undergo. Moreover, the end-result of the servanthood of Israel remains unchanged: it is still intended that all people, the "many," the "masses of humankind," may be won, like Ruth the Gentile, into the joy of the covenant God has intended all people to enjoy. So it is now not merely Israel who is portrayed as the servant to this end; in this ideal calling it is God's Spirit that has taken the place of Israel's ego and which is now dwelling in Israel's flesh. Even the heathen can see this clearly: "Verily God is *in* you only," they say. "In fact, thou, the Savior God of Israel, hidest thyself" (in this way). <u>In other words, God works in the</u> <u>world as the world's Savior by hiding in the flesh of the covenant people.</u> That is why chapter 53 ends as it does, even as it announces the effective power of the martyrdom of the servant. For it is the Spirit of God, *in* Israel, and through the sufferings of the *human* Israel, that triumphs over pain and death, and thus effects that which we have seen the servant was called to effect, the salvation of the "many." In a word, "The will of the Lord shall prosper in his hand." Genesis 1:1-3 had already expressed this reality in a nutshell. It is not the *essence* of God that is revealed to the eye of man, it is the *will* of God.

Out of the chaos in which Israel now dwelt in Exile, then, as a mere scattering of dry bones over the Euphrates valley, God effected a resurrection. He did so, first, *in history*, when his Messiah, Cyrus, "set the prisoners free" (Isa. 45:1-7), and Israel returned to Zion to rebuild her ancient home (Ezra 1). For God's salvation is of this earth, earthy. But, second, he did so in order that that human element in his creation, the covenant people whom he had chosen, might be his instrument to *keep on recreating* (we remember the active participial form of this unique verb) through forgiveness and the potency of love the whole of humankind whom God has set on this earth.

CHAPTER 7

Apocalyptic and Eschatology

*T*HERE IS A WHOLE AREA OF THOUGHT THAT IS UNIQUE TO Israel, one that differentiates the I AM of the Old Testament from all the gods and religions of man. This is that for centuries Israel entertained no concept of a life after death. The result was that she held a very different relationship to God from that of the world's religions.

It is surprising that Israel could emerge from Egypt in the days of Moses without being in the least affected by Egypt's thought. The majestic pyramids were already some 1500 years old when Moses gazed at them. Whatever they were meant to be besides housing a tomb, they undoubtedly pointed to belief in a life beyond. We have inherited Egypt's guidebook to the world beyond the grave, its *Book of the Dead*. Egypt not only worshipped 80 gods in Moses' day, but she also knew all about their functions on both sides of death.

A Near Eastern grave was excavated a generation ago in which were found the king arrayed in all his finery, surrounded by his wives and courtiers, together with their horses and even their chariots. So, too, with others of Israel's contemporaries; they all lived in this world of pain and sorrow just in order to die.

The early Greeks, of course, had their ideas about how the souls of the dead had to be ferried across the river Styx to reach the gloom of Hades. In abandoning their inherited myths, however, the philosophers and poets of Greece did not give up belief in the immortality of the soul. The religious quest of the ancient world of that period was curiously one. Plato and Aristotle were informed in a general sort of way about the thought of Persia, with its dualism, and of India, with its pantheism. Thus there was one unifying belief that was held as axiomatic by virtually all people, and that has persisted to this day in the Eastern religions; it is a belief in the immortality of the soul. Even today modern secular man supposes that a belief in the immortality of the soul is a basic doctrine of the Christian Faith, despite the fact that the idea finds no place in any of the creeds of Christendom. Thus it is that the Judaeo-Christian faith cannot possibly entertain such speculative ideas as that of the transmigration of souls, nor conceive that it is possible, through a medium, to converse with the souls of the dead. Why should all this be so, we may well ask, and why did Israel's God, *I AM with you*, not create man with an immortal soul?

J's picture of the constitution of man, found at Genesis 2:7, is that he is compounded from the soil. This is of course correct, in that man is what he eats, and everything that he eats—whether meat, vegetables, grains, or fruit—comes out of the ground. Into this creaturely effigy God then breathed life. Man thus became a living *nephesh*. In this passage God does not "give man a soul." He does not set within him a *scintilla dei*, a spark of the divine. He creates man to be of the earth, earthy, and so, being dust, to dust will man return.

The King James Version does not understand the Hebrew here. For 2000 years our Western culture has been created by the interplay of the two strands of which it has been composed—our Greek and our Hebraic heritages. We owe so much to both. But there has often been an imbalance between them. Today, for example, in those countries where you have a secular school system, children are taught that our democracy stems from Greece. Such instruction is ideological dogmatism. Children ought to be taught to look up the original source material for themselves. Actually Greek democratic ideals lead directly to the apartheid system of South Africa. If they were allowed to do so, however, by examining the Old Testament children could discover that the system whereby the elder acted as a kind of Justice of the Peace in his village and represented his village when he went up to Jerusalem three times a year to the great festivals goes back to 1000 B.C.; on such occasions he conferred with the powers that be, whether king or high priest, and so began the line that reaches to and eventuates in our Westminster understanding of popular representation. The Greeks were notorious for their racial prejudice, their dependence on slavery, their scorn of marriage and of the value of women, and their acceptance of homosexuality as a way of life. Who in a secular school today is invited to turn to the Old Testament to discover that Moses took to himself a black wife? With this Greek heritage as axiomatic, and today held with a scornful imbalance in relation to a study of our Hebraic heritage, the complementarity of the male-female relationship that we find clearly expressed in any modern translation of Genesis 2:18, 23-24 has not been found completely acceptable either in the period when the KJV was translated or in today's Western world. This deliberate dogmatic evasion of the second strand of our culture has caused untold harm in man-woman relationships. The present-day flirtation by Westerners with the Eastern way of life has come about through the fact that the Greeks were allies of the East without recognizing what they were doing. Yet the Hebraic strand in our culture stands out in stark contrast to both Greek and Hindu culture. For one thing, it lays primary stress on the family as the basic unit in society, deplores the homosexuality that Plato exalted, and sets the woman as queen of the home.

Again, the Greeks are said to be the fathers of history writing. Yet five hundred years before Herodotus was born an anonymous author had produced the court history of David, written in a manner as compelling as that of any Greek historian. But between the Greek and the Hebrew writer lies that one point of difference which marks the essential uniqueness of Old Testament thinking. The Greek writers, despite their ability to tell a story and to show relationships between cause and effect, failed to discover any *meaning* in the events they described. This was because the Greeks possessed no fixed point outside of history to which they could refer the relative nature of the flow of events. They were therefore never able to suggest where events were leading to. When he reached the end of a war, the historian laid down his pen. That story had been told; now to the next. But the biblical historians were not primarily concerned to tell a tale that could be analyzed with the intent of discovering "what actually happened." Compare the report left to us of the fall of Jericho in the book of Joshua. The author of that book was concerned to show that history was in the hands of *I AM with you*, that history had a meaning, and that all that happened was leading forward to an ultimate goal. It is only those who have been indoctrinated by the teaching they have received in their secular schooling in this generation, which reflects the ideological slant that ignores the Hebraic half of our Western cultural heritage, who could fall into the trap of supposing that the God whom the Old Testament knows as *I AM with you* could ever be known by any other name and yet remain I AM.

We return now to the word *nephesh*, which we introduced above. We have noted that "the Greeks," like the Eastern mystics, split reality in two. From the view that there is the world of the senses and there is the world of the ideal, they developed the idea that man, too, is a duality. He is body and he is soul. The soul dwells within the body, but at death it is released from its "tomb," as some philosophers regarded the body to be. As late as three hundred years ago a group of doctors requested a dying man to allow them to weigh him just before and just after he had breathed his last in order to discover the weight of his soul.

The word *nephesh*, then, does not mean "soul" as the Greek-Hindu world thinks of it. Because of the weight of our Greek heritage pressing on us disproportionately in our Western culture, we do not possess one particular word to express the Hebrew here. *Nephesh* describes the total personality of a person—in fact, all that we today seek to analyze into body, soul, and spirit. The Psalmist even equates his person with his kidneys! (Jeremiah 11:20 is an example of this.) Even more than that, this word describes what a person is in relation to his environment, to his parents, his spouse, his children, his friends, his neighbors, and even his cultural setting. For no man is an island. Israel came out of Egypt with no concept of an individual "soul" that, at death, would continue to exist as an entity in its own right. A "soul," a *nephesh*, was a physical body. It was a "member, " a limb—like a finger on a hand—of a corporate group, all of which was informed by the breath of God; and all members of this corporate body were called to live out the meaning and purpose of God's will in their common life. In the Old Testament this group was called the people of God. In the New Testament it became known as the body of Christ. Moreover, it was *in this world* that the group was called to be God's kingdom of priests, God's witnesses, God's servant, God's son, God's light, the medium of God's saving purpose.

We hear the Psalmist cry for justice to be done *here and now*. He did this because, unless it was done now, it would never be done. For this world is the *place* of God's redeeming love, and thus it is the *place* where God will grant his *shalom*, his peace, security, and wholeness of life when "the day of the Lord" dawns. When it does, the wolf will dwell with the lamb, and the lion will eat straw like the ox. "Then all wars shall cease, and men shall beat their swords into plowshares, and their spears into pruning hooks." Then, too, every man and his family will dwell in *shalom* under his own vine and under his own fig-tree, and live on in glorious security to a ripe old age.

But the question of *meaning* kept pressing in on Israel's view of the ways of God in her life. The basic cry of Ecclesiastes, the Preacher, was: "What is the meaning of life?" Yet his answer, "There is none, there is only meaninglessness," represents that "chaos" in human thinking which God actually employs to create what is new and ultimately complete.

As early as the preaching of the prophet Amos in the mid-eighth century B.C. we can discern the beginnings of what we label today "apocalyptic"—a "lifting of the lid" off history, to discover, in picture language, what history is all about, and where it is all leading. We find apocalyptic writing again in the book of Isaiah. Chapter 27 begins with "In that day the Lord with his cruel and powerful sword will punish Leviathan the fleeing serpent, Leviathan the twisting serpent, and he will slay the dragon that is in the sea." 25:6 reads: "On this mountain [Zion] the Lord of hosts will make for all peoples a feast of fat things. . . . And he will destroy on this mountain the covering that is cast over all peoples. . . . He will swallow up death for ever."

The book of Daniel uses apocalyptic explicitly: "As for the fourth beast, there shall be a fourth kingdom on earth. . . . But the kingdom and the dominion . . . shall be given to the people of the saints of the Most High" (Dan. 8:23, 27). In this way, and once again by means of picture language, apocalyptic seeks to portray the *end* of history, just as the Genesis Prologue, also in pictures, showed its very beginning. The two together seek to express the total meaning of the plan of God.

Yet apocalyptic, either in the Old Testament or in the New (see, for example, 1 Thess. 4:15-17), does not offer us the final answer to the question of meaning. It is only a halfway house to help our poor, inadequate human understanding as we try to grasp what reality is. Apocalyptic has been given us as a temporary aid "for the hardness of your hearts," as Jesus put it (Matt. 19:8; Mark 10:5) with reference to that other halfway house, the Law of Moses. The answer we are looking for, however, is to be found in what we now label eschatology.

That word means "having to do with the last things." But so had apocalyptic. Yet apocalyptic was only a borrowing from the pagan mode of thought that shows itself in the religions of the world. Even the idea of Sheol as a dimly lit area of semi-existence after death was a borrowing from the neighboring peoples. It was soon rejected by the prophets and the Psalmists, and used, just as God uses chaos, to create a whole new way of thinking about the significance of death. Eschatology, unlike apocalyptic, did not have to do with religion; it had to do with meaning. Once again, interestingly enough, the fullness of the mystery contained in that word came to light in the works of Deutero-Isaiah.

We recall that he was one of the exiles in Babylon. His message was that the period of Israel's "forced labor" (Isa. 40:2) was ended. God was now about to send his Messiah, King Cyrus, to "let my people go." Cyrus would soon release the "captives" from the prison gangs of Babylon, bringing them forth from the darkness of the underground civic works in the basements of public buildings on which they were deployed, and set them completely free. They would then be resurrected (to use Ezekiel's fascinating picture in chap. 37 of his book) and be able to return to their ancient and beloved home, to Zion. And this they actually did. It is a fact of history that they did so. We read of it in Ezra's memoirs; and his story is confirmed in the Persian annals.

But Deutero-Isaiah recognized that God's loving, saving action *in history* was more than a mere historical happening. It was actually a moment of revelation of what the eternal God is eternally like, the God whose name is *I AM with you*. This revelation therefore opens up to our understanding what God is always doing, both in the past when he redeemed Israel out of Egypt, and at that time when Deutero-Isaiah was acting as a "voice." But it means even more. God's historical action when he employed King Cyrus as his Messiah was such that all previous redemptive acts would be forgotten in comparison with the extraordinary new thing he was about to do. In the beginning God had used chaos in the form of flood as his instrument for producing the good. He had used the waters in the days of Noah to give the earth a new beginning (Isa. 54:9). The waters of the Red Sea, in the same way, had represented the floods of the waters under the earth. They were *there*, as historical fact, and if they had not been there, then the redemption of Israel would not have been seen to have taken place. So now, the redemption from Babylon was to be seen finally as a token, a memorial (that is, a reminder), of God's actions as a going beyond history into eternity. "Instead of the thorn shall come up the cypress," and so will the briar, which grows in the wilderness of chaos—*it* (*sic!*) shall become the name of the Lord, an everlasting sign or reminder, which shall never be abrogated (Isa. 55:13).

The redemption from Babylon would now be the outward and visible sign of what God is eternally like in himself, the Redeemer, the Savior, the *I AM with you*. "When you pass through the waters *I am with you*" (Isa. 43:2). Apocalyptic had sought to express the meaning of God's purposes within creation, within the realm we may designate either as heaven, or as purgatory, or as the place of departed souls. But such a place would still be part of creation, part of the "heavens" that God had created and therefore still part of creation, even though hidden from our eyes. Eschatology, on the other hand, expresses, not what apocalyptic seeks to portray, but what God is eternally like in himself, both *now*, when Israel passes through the waters of affliction, and also *then*, at the *end*, at the *eschaton*. Such, however, will be true only because, at the end, God will still be the same as he is now.[1]

This new view of reality, given us by Deutero-Isaiah, has remained uniquely in our Judaeo-Christian faith over against all the religions of the world. It has taught us that *now* is not just a fleeting moment. *Now* is something that is eternally significant. "Now," says Paul, "is the day of salvation"—not in another life or in the beyond. Each moment we live is of eschatological significance, the whole of Scripture declares; each choice we make, each victory won, each act of kindness done is an eternal act—for we do it unto him. It is as if life could be viewed as a coin. A coin is one entity, not two, but it has two sides. On one side we may observe a local emblem, representing the kind of life we know in our particular country. It belongs to space and time. If we belong to the British Commonwealth of nations, however, what we find on the back of the coin is the Queen's head. Thus the back of the coin reminds us, not of where we live, but of the quality of life that obtains in such a united Commonwealth, and of its complex of hopes, aspirations, and joys. You cannot see the two sides of a coin at once. Consequently a Comonwealth coin may be preserved in a glass case with the Queen's head not in view. The existence of the latter is assumed by faith alone. But conversely the visible side, with its signs and symbols, becomes the great sign that will never be abrogated (Isa. 55:13).

Thus we come to discover that whatever we do, here and now, in our lifespan of three score years and ten, is of eternal significance. "I tell you," says Jesus, "on the day of judgment men will render account for every careless word they utter." This world is no vale of tears; nor is it *maya*, illusion. It is

1. See my "Eschatology in the Old Testament," *Scottish Journal of Theology*, IV (1951), 355–62. It is now also in German, in the volume *Eschatologie im Alten Testament* (1978), pp. 22–30.

God's creation—"and God saw that it was good." This is just what the "angel of the Lord" said of the newborn baby Jesus, that he was of eschatological significance (Matt. 1:21), and what Simeon implied in his expression of complete satisfaction (Luke 2:30-32). Jesus answered those Sadducees who doubted the resurrection by using this same category of thought which we find in the Old Testament. Just as today many honest doubters reject what they *think* Christianity is because they imagine it to be just one of the religions of the world, so with those sincere Sadducees. They rejected the idea of the continuing existence of the human soul beyond death, for they recognized such to be a concept of pagan origin. Jesus in his reply referred them back to our basic text at Exodus 3:15, to the words I AM. It is foolish, he taught, ever to put the question to another person, "Do you believe in life after death?" This is a question the Gentiles ask, he might have added. For the life of the human soul is not something that exists in its own right apart from God who gave it. What he did was to remind the Sadducees of God's "real presence"with Abraham, Isaac, and Jacob. That real presence must still be real, he implies; or otherwise it is not the presence of the real God. Consequently Abraham is still there in the presence of the great I AM. Jesus repeats the same point in his parable of the Last Judgment (Matt. 25:31-46). There he shows how that moment when we visit the sick, or feed the hungry, is the last moment we could ever do so. If we wait an hour before acting, the situation has changed. The hungry man may no longer be there. That moment therefore is eternal. Even giving a cup of cold water to a thirsty man is eschatologically significant; what is more, the very act of doing so is the moment that we "enter into eternal life" (v. 46).

All this, then, must be taken into account before we pronounce judgments in the area of the study of the Phenomenology of Religion and of Comparative Religion. Not only, may it be said, when we do so in the *study* of these sciences, but much more particularly in the *teaching* of them. In other words, and to sum up thus far, dare we lead young minds even to consider whether the great I AM is in fact a God with many names?

CHAPTER 8

Immanuel

*T*HE BIBLICAL FAITH, THEN, IS CENTERED ON LIFE ON THIS earth, as we know it now. In fact, despite all that we have said so far, it is finally centered on one man. This man was born into the heritage we have now outlined. He was born into the ancient covenant. He was an Israelite. He was a member of that people of whom God had said, "Israel is my son, my first-born son," to whom, as Paul adds, "God had revealed his glory, had given the Law, the worship, and the promises" (Rom. 9:4). Thus Jesus was not born as a mere isolated individual, within the disorganized (that is to say, not possessing the divine *shalom*) society of Greece or Persia. He was the epitome, the indigenization, the "explicitation" of the divine activity that works through the Covenant that had been in progress since the foundation of the world; ever since, in fact, God had said, "Let there be light, and light became"; ever since God had said, "I establish my covenant with you"(Gen. 9:9); ever since God had said to Abraham "Go" and Abraham went, and God went with him; ever since God had said to Moses, "Go into that chaos which is Egyptian society, and bring out my people Israel"and had then added the words, "It is I AM who is sending you, the I AM who will be *with* you always."

This "with-ness" of the I AM with his world in covenant is what we ultimately call the Incarnation. The record of this activity of God we find even before the birth of Jesus. First we read, "An angel of the Lord appeared to Joseph in a dream, saying, 'Joseph, son of David . . .' " (Matt. 2:20). The child to be born, then, was a son of King David, who was himself a special son of God. All Israel was of course the corporate son

49

of God. But at the same time, this representative of Israel to God and of God to Israel was also God's son in a special way. "I will be his father, and he shall be my son," as God had said to David through his prophet Nathan, with reference to the whole line of kings to come (2 Sam. 7:14). The people of Israel had entered into awareness of this mystery with joy and acclamation, as we see from such Psalms as 2, 45, 72, 110, and 132. This son was the "anointed," the Messiah, God's vicegerent on earth (Acts 4:25-26). At his baptism at the hand of John the Baptist, Jesus, in turn, became intensely aware of this mystery: "And lo, a voice from heaven [the Jewish expression, a *bath qol*, a sudden consciousness of God's working in one's heart], saying, 'This is my beloved son,' " "beloved" being the Greek translation of the Hebrew "firstborn" when it referred to the election of all Israel.

We continue at Matthew 2:20. "Do not fear to take Mary your wife, for that which is conceived in her is of the Holy Spirit." So God is still working in the same way as he was in the beginning. For then the Spirit, this mother element in the eternal I AM, just as a bird who broods over her eggs to create life therefrom, had brooded over chaos, and so light was born! So now there was born he of whom John's Gospel could declare, "I AM the light of the world."

But who was this Mary, this mother here? She was the one representative of all Israel whom God himself, in accordance with his plan, had chosen to give birth to this child. How do we know this about Mary? Naturally it is to the Old Testament that we return to discover the answer; for we keep in mind that there is only one biblical theology, and that is Old Testament theology.

Hosea first, and then after him Jeremiah, had illustrated the covenant relationship between God and Israel as that between Husband and Bride. By so doing these prophets had revealed the otherwise unspeakably deep and wonderful relationship between God and his chosen people that only the pure and grateful love of a woman for a good man can illustrate. But even before Hosea's day Amos, to be followed by the poems in the book of Lamentations, had used the theological picture of Israel as God's Virgin Daughter.

Finally, Trito-Isaiah took up the analogy. He was writing after the "resurrection" of Israel, when they were back home in Zion, that female city which represented the female people of God. He spoke of her as being in labor, until finally she was delivered of a son (Isa. 66:7). The father of this child, born from the womb of the Virgin People of God, could only be God himself, for God alone was her Husband, according to the thought of the great prophets who had gone before. This birth then had to become reality, as Isaiah 66:9 puts it. This was because the child must be born in accordance with the will of him who was using the babe to work out his plan for the redemption of the world.

Not that God's plan was confined to this one birth, for all Israel was God's sons (Isa. 66:8). But then Israel was God's corporate son (and daughters too!) as Paul asserts in Acts 6:16-18, where he puts together a number of Old Testament quotations. As God's corporate son, Israel was represented by one who was Head of the body. And so this child is to be born of the Holy Spirit, that Spirit which was present in the womb of time, and now again in the womb of the Virgin People of God, as they were represented by one woman. Knowing that the truth of the gospel is beyond rational analysis, neither Testament is reluctant to express God's ways in figurative speech or in pictorial theology.

We continue with Matthew 2:21: "She will bear a son." No child can be born unless the marriage is first consummated. This consummation is what old Simeon had been looking for (Luke 2:25). The English word "consolation" refers to that moment when the divine Husband should take his beloved Bride to himself, and, through the Holy Spirit, consummate the marriage by becoming "one flesh" with her, thus "consummating" his covenant relationship with Israel. Isaiah 62:4 had expressed the certainty that a *physical* union would one day take place between God and Israel. Such language meant no less than that the Holy Spirit would unite in a creative manner with the Bride. Thus it was that, when the child of that union was born, his nature was such that he could be hailed as being both Son of God and Son of Man at the same time.

We continue. "And you will call his name Jesus, for he will save his people from their sins." "Jesus" is *Je-hoshua‘*, or "Yahweh is Savior." Jesus is not simply the Savior. Medieval scholars, not knowing Hebrew, often found themselves in great theological trouble at this point. They had forgotten this declaration: "I, I am Yahweh, and besides me there is no savior" (Isa. 43:11). Yet a new situation had now taken place. God's all-comprehensive purpose, that of bringing the world out of its chaos into his marvelous *shalom*, has now begun to take root in space and time in the body of a human being. This human person will now incarnate the saving love of the I AM and in himself effect the saving purpose of Almighty God. As Paul put it succinctly: "God was *in* Christ, reconciling the world to himself" (2 Cor. 5:19). We have already noted the basic statement of Deutero-Isaiah from the lips of Gentiles, that God was *in* Israel (Isa. 45:14). Thus the "he" in the clause "he will save his people from their sins" refers to Yahweh. This people is his own people from the first days of the Covenant, his Beloved, his Bride. And now she is the Mother of his Son.

Matthew 1:22 continues: "All this took place to fulfil what Yahweh [the I AM] had spoken by the prophet:

'Behold a virgin shall conceive and bear a son,
And his name shall be called Emmanuel' (which means
     'God with us')."

In the meaning of this word, better spelled Immanuel, is summed up the promise made to Moses of "I AM, or, I will be, with you." The basic Semitic name for the Divine Being is *’el*, a word that we render by "God." At Exodus 6:2-3 P's retelling of the event recorded in Exodus 3 is expressed this way: "I am Yahweh; I appeared to Abraham, to Isaac, and to Jacob as God Almighty [*’el shaddai*], but in the form of my name Yahweh I did not make myself known to them." What we have in Matthew's quotation from Isaiah 7:14 therefore makes reference to the above idea but now in the third person: "God with us" is what the name Immanuel means. However, we have to add the word "is" in order to express the phrase in proper English.

This child grows up to be a man. Yet there is one aspect of

his manhood that sets him off from all the other sons of man. He asks this question of his best friends, "Who is there to accuse me of sin?" As we read the Gospels, without hearing a word said by anyone on the issue, we notice how, in all the contacts he makes with all kinds of men and women, he never reflects the egoism and self-centeredness that is characteristic of every human being. On the contrary, what we witness is a creative activity flowing from his words and actions that heals, forgives, sustains, comforts, and recreates other people—to the extent, we might even suggest, that he has no time left to heal himself. We are amazed to see his singleness of purpose, his simplicity, his purity of heart, his deep compassion (we read that "his bowels moved within him" at the sight of a dirty blind man), his complete seriousness about the reality of God and about taking God at his word. He would not have been like this, of course, if he had known sin, as Hebrews 4:15 reminds us. It is sin that raises the barrier between the creative love of God and what the human person can do in his name, not the weakness of the flesh. The latter belongs in the realm of the physical, of the matter that God created and saw that it was good for his purpose. So God can still do with the created body as he wills; he can recreate it, the four Gospels believe, because the body is no tomb. That was a notion current in Jesus' day among the educated people of the Roman Empire. And so the last verses of all four Gospels come really as no surprise.

Much scholarly discussion has gone on about the origin and meaning of the title that Jesus gave to himself. He spoke of himself as Son of Man, a title no one else gave him. What then did he imply by doing so? We have already seen, when discussing the name I AM, how important to the people of the Bible the name was. Most of the discussion on the title Son of Man, however, has been in the area of archaeological and philological research, and not in the area of theology. Jesus spoke Aramaic, and in that language the term could be a polite substitute for the pronoun "I." That may have been an element in Jesus' use of the term that appealed to his deep humility and forgetfulness of self. On the other hand, scholars have discovered the title in sources outside of the Bible. But I am sure that the carpenter of Nazareth who had been educated only in the village synagogue school and later in discussions with rabbis whose whole field of experience was the Old Testament only, would know absolutely nothing of the literature where this name appears. Where then did Jesus find this term used in the Old Testament? And what meaning did it convey in this literature he knew so well that he could take it and apply it to himself?

(1) Jesus found that God had used the term as a form of address when he spoke directly to one particular man, and one only. This one man was the prophet Ezekiel. He was the first of the prophets living in the Exile who found themselves giving a theological meaning to events. "Son of man, stand upon your feet, and I will speak with you" (Ezek. 2:1). In a word, it would seem that God respected this prophet as a real man, one *with* whom he could confidently speak his mind and reveal to him an interpretation of coming events. It looks as if Ezekiel was able to give his full attention, ability, and strength to listen to what God had to say. Ezekiel could stand erect, hear, and then obey. God had created Ezekiel to do, in some sense, what he himself does, namely, create. Ezekiel was given the task of interpreting and of conveying God's plan to recreate his people Israel. Yet, as Ezekiel was only a man, he had to place himself in a position where he could only interpret what the Savior God was doing in the life of the world, and let his people know of it.

(2) The term Son of Man is a name for all Israel, "the man of thy right hand, the son of man whom thou hast made strong for thyself" (raised up to be a strong son—Ps. 80:17). But, as we have seen, Israel's task was to do in relation to humankind exactly what Ezekiel's task was in relation to his own people, Israel.

(3) Israel in the Old Testament is a corporate personality. Daniel 7, which Jesus quotes, speaks of the Israel that is to be as "one like a son of man, and he came to the Ancient of Days and was presented before him. And to him was given dominion and glory and kingdom, that all peoples, nations, and languages should serve him. . . . And the kingdom and the dominion and the greatness of the kingdoms under the whole

heaven shall be given to the people of the saints of the Most High." This people Israel, this corporate son of man, was always represented before God by one "head" of the body politic. Thus it was that when God said to Moses, "I will be with you," he was saying those words to all Israel. We noted this when we looked at Isaiah 43:2. In the same way God could address all Israel by confronting that chronologically later head of the body, namely, King David. This apocalyptic, Danielic language may well be what Jesus had in mind when he declared: "And then they will see the Son of Man coming in clouds with great power and glory. And then he will send out the angels, and gather his elect from the four winds" (Mark 13:26-27, as in all three Synoptic Gospels).

(4) Psalm 8:4 equates "man" with "son of man." If Jesus made use of this verse, then he was implying that he is typical man. Yet typical not in the sense that he is a rebel against God, like Cain the son of man (Adam), but as one who senses in awe the mystery of God's ways, as a person must do when he is confronted with the power of God (Ps. 143:3). This understanding of Psalm 8 is underlined still more when we notice that the word for "man" in it is not Adam, but Enosh, the kind of humanity with which God began to fill the earth all over again after the line of Cain had ended with the disaster of Lamech. It was only when God created this new line of humanity that "men began to call upon the name of the Lord" (Gen. 4:23-26), or, more accurately, "It was begun to invoke Yahweh by *name*."

(5) Yet Enosh was as truly son of Adam as was Cain. The plan of God in first creating Adam, that is, humankind (both male and female—Gen. 1:26-27), was that man should be able to do what God does, namely, create. For surely, to be in the image of God means to do what God does. We have seen that nowhere in the Bible are we mortals given an understanding of what I AM is in himself. Revelation in the Bible is measured to suit our limited grasp, not of what Reality is, but of what God does, as he acts, creates, and recreates. To be created in God's image, therefore, is to be fashioned to do just that; when God says "I AM with you," therefore, he is revealing himself as the divine creative

power who engages to help "you" to do what he does.

The reality of all this moved out of the area of theology into practical human living at one particular moment in history and within the experience of but one people out of all the nations of the earth, and as the final episode in the particular act of God known as the Incarnation. We have declared that God reveals himself as the "divine creative power who engages to help 'you' to do what he does." Throughout the centuries this creative power was known under the designation the Spirit of God. But once the revelation of God's creative love was finally particularized, that is, made flesh at one point in history, that creative love was passed on and transferred to those of the ancient covenant people who had now been called to accept this revelation for themselves and to act on it for the world. Luke reports that the risen Christ declared to his disciples: "And behold, I send the promise of my Father upon you; but stay in the city [very particular this!] until you are clothed with power from on high" (Luke 24:49). They did stay in the city until they were clothed from on high ("high," even the sun and the moon having something to do with it—Acts 2:20) with the power of creative love. Luke called this event Pentecost after the exact moment in history at which it happened. It is natural that since God is all in all, the gifts of his Spirit should be many and various. But there is evidently one unifying and comprehensive gift, according to Paul at 1 Corinthians 12:31–13:13, and that is the love that we experience in Christ.

The Hebrew word *ḥesed*, used throughout the Old Testament to describe what the RSV translates by "steadfast love" within the covenant that endures forever (e.g., Ps. 136), is linked with several other Hebrew words that describe the manner in which God loves, both as a Father and as a Mother, to produce that concept of love which Paul calls *agape* in Greek, and which he struggles to describe in 1 Corinthians 13. "Struggles," we say, because love is of God. It was the God who said to Moses "I AM with you" who himself gave this kind of love to his covenant people at Pentecost; that is to say, this divine creative love is not of this world; for it is not a human invention. But through this power of love, "We hear," declare the nations, "each of us in his own native language . . . the mighty works of God." These "mighty works" are of course God's creative acts of love.

"In the beginning of God's creating. . . ," however, there was chaos. Man, as part of creation, is involved in that chaos. Man chooses freely to reject God's offer of creative love, which he could have possessed in obedience to God. Consequently he must be expelled from the Garden (Gen. 3). But if God created man in his own image before the Fall described in Genesis 3, before man knew what it meant to rebel, and so before man became a sinner, then is not this Jesus who called himself Son of Adam (Man) not the son of the Adam whom God made in his own image? Can this Jesus not say without fear of contradiction, "He who has seen me has seen the Father"?

Jesus then called himself Son of Man, the summation of the election of Israel, and the Head of the body of the people of God. Yet he was more, if our argument above is valid. He was also very man, true man, representative man; and since he was man without sin, he was virtually claiming that he was *able* to do in obedience what God does, namely, recreate. To recreate, however, is merely another verb for to save.

By his choice of term, then, Jesus goes behind all racial, religious, social, and cultural distinctions. The Hindu is man—but so is Jesus. The Sikh is man—but so is Jesus. The Marxist is man—but so is Jesus. You cannot insert the *man* Jesus into the Hindu pantheon, for it is only gods who can fit in there. You cannot fit the *man* Jesus into a Marxist ideology, for man made in the image of God is free and creative, as was Enosh, and is able to "invoke Yahweh by name." You cannot adopt Jesus into a humanist pattern for a well-ordered and ideal human society, because Jesus is free to be astonished at the glory of God, as was Enosh in Psalm 8—free to judge, condemn, and recreate that humanist order no matter what form it takes.

The Hebrew idiom "son of . . . " has two meanings. (1) It has the literal sense of "John is the son of Andrew and Margaret." (2) It represents a peculiarly Semitic way of speaking (very obvious in Arabic usage). Thus, Jesus could call James and John "sons of thunder" (Mark 3:17), or Judas "the son of perdition" (John 17:12). In Old Testament times the local bullyboys could be described as "sons of Belial" (e.g., Judg. 19:22). These youthful thugs were doing the opposite of what God does; they were destroying, whereas God creates. While the word Belial may possibly mean "worthless," it may also be the name of some evil spirit. This usage of "son of . . . " then points to how a man could be a representative of, or be filled with the spirit of violence of a thunderstorm, or of a destructive gang, or of perdition itself. Consequently, this usage shows us that the term Son of Man, which Jesus used of himself and which *no one else* ever used of him, must include within it the idea that Jesus was representative man, the essence of man, and so man made in the image of God.

But we are not finished yet with the term "son of man." At his trial it was a man who stood before Pilate. The latter, pagan as he was, perhaps somewhat attracted to the religion known as Mithraism that was popular among the Roman soldiers of his day, involuntarily exclaimed, "Behold, a man!" Mithraism held all kinds of odd ideas about semi-divine beings. This man, however, Pilate knew intuitively, was a real man, although this Jesus who stood before him bore every mark of human degradation. *Ecce homo*, said Pilate in his own language, not necessarily to be translated "*the* man," or "Here is the man" (John 19:5 RSV); for the Latin language employs no article; so it may simply be "Behold, a *man*!" The Greek of this verse does employ the definite article, but its usage is idiomatic, and so could mean "Behold, humanity!" Thus it might be understood to mean "Behold, a real man at last!" It was because of this overwhelming conviction of the integrity of this man, therefore, that another Roman, watching a *man* die, could exclaim, "Truly this was a son of *God*!" (Mark 15:39). This Gentile centurion knew nothing of the background of this man on the cross, nothing at all of God's mighty works that had taken place in the life of that first son of God, namely, Israel (Exod. 4:22-23). But those who did know Jesus' background, those who believed that God had long planned for the coming of such a one, began almost at once to call him, not *a* son of God, but *the* Son of God, that is to say, one who fully represents on earth the eternal recreative work of God.

So finally we note that Jesus' own deliberate choice of name for himself, Son of Man, helps us to define what the Incarnation means without finding ourselves in metaphysical deep waters. For one thing, Jesus never accepted the title people sought to thrust on him, when they hailed him as God's choice of leader, one who was expected under the title of Messiah. Cyrus the mighty warrior had received that name. David the warrior-king had been hailed as that also. Nor did Jesus ever acknowledge explicitly the title Son of God. To have done so would have been contrary to his refusal to grasp at equality with God. Thus the relationship between the Son and the Father, in the Synoptic Gospels, is never defined in ways that would lead us to use language about "essence" and the like. We know nothing about what the phrase "the essence of the Godhead" can mean, and we never shall be able to know. What Jesus lets us see, on the other hand, is that on earth, in a real man, God *does* what it is God's nature to do. And so we can come to the final conclusion, that Jesus reveals to the eyes of people within space and time the reality of the eternal Holy Trinity (Matt. 28:18-20). In a word, in the Synoptic Gospels the concept of "God" is revealed in terms of the function of the Godhead, and not of its essence. Yet to dare use that latter word for a moment, Jesus shows that the essence of the Godhead, of the Holy Trinity, can be revealed to our eyes when we see him emptying himself of all that could be described by means of human names and titles, even as God himself has revealed himself by means of a name that is in fact no name at all.

CHAPTER 9

Doom and Resurrection

WHILE THE SYNOPTIC GOSPELS SHOW US JESUS EMPTYING himself to become the servant of servants, the two great New Testament theologians, Paul and John, go their own separate ways to interpret him as they had found him to be, both in their own lives and in the life of the Church. At times Paul uses cosmic language to describe him. This is because he seeks to express the reality that greatness and power are not visible in terms of egoism and bloodthirstiness. Paul's language about Christ, however, is without exception taken from the Old Testament. So we read: "He has delivered us from the dominion of darkness and transferred us to the kingdom of his beloved Son, in whom we have redemption, the forgiveness of sins. He is the image of the invisible God, the first-born of all creation; for in him all things were created, in heaven and on earth, visible and invisible, whether thrones or dominions or principalities or authorities—all things were created through him and for him. He is before all things, and in him all things hold together. He is the head of the body, the church; he is the beginning, the first-born from the dead, that in everything he might be preeminent. For in him all the fullness of God was pleased to dwell" (Col. 1:13-19).

It would be wise for us, however, to concentrate on just one element in this vast subject, both to keep this book within limits and to discover that even one of the many elements in Old Testament revelation that have been adopted by the New Testament is sufficient for our understanding of the meaning of the Incarnation. That element is Jesus' use of the words I AM that is the "name" of the God of the Old Testament. The Synoptic Gospels report Jesus as saying "I am" on a number of occasions in a normal grammatical manner. Thus, at Matthew 24:5 we have, "For many will come in my name, saying, 'I am the Christ.' " And Mark 14:61 reads, "The high priest asked him, 'Are you the Christ, the Son of the Blessed?' And Jesus said, 'I am.' " The words used in the last clause are *ego eimi*. In this latter case, however, Jesus' answer *could* be understood on two levels. The double possibility is observable again at Mark 6:50, in the incident in which Jesus came walking on the "sea" to the disciples, and they were afraid. Then Jesus declared, "Don't be afraid, *ego eimi*." In this instance it looks as if the story sought to make clear that Jesus was doing at that moment what God had done in the beginning when he brought calm and peace out of the stormy *tehōm*, the primal watery chaos. But, as we have said, the Synoptic Gospels do not demand such an interpretation, though at times they are ambivalent about it.

The many "I am's" of the Fourth Gospel, however, seem to be explicit interpretations of who this Jesus is. In the Fourth Gospel we actually hear John employing the ambivalent language of Jesus' own words found in the Synoptic Gospels, in such a manner that he seems to have turned the words of Jesus into pictorial theology. He does so by using the kind of language that maintains and exegetes similar usages in the Old Testament.

John does not discuss the question of the preexistence of Jesus that modern theologians feel obliged to raise. To have done so would have been merely to speculate in an area not revealed to our sight, namely, the essence of the Godhead. John reports on how Jesus keeps to the area of function, that function which has already been revealed, namely, *"I AM with you;* this is my *name* for ever."* So when we hear the words "I AM" from Jesus' lips in the Fourth Gospel, for example, "Before Abraham was, I AM" (John 8:58), we discover that John is declaring that from the beginning Jesus had been doing what God does, namely, love and save and recreate. The question as John deals with it is simply not a metaphysical one at all. It is not a statement about Christ's essential preexistence, but is one reminding us that the Word is the same yesterday, today, and forever. It reminds us that the Word was with the Israelites when they came forth out of the "chaos" of the social situation in which they lived under the lash of the taskmaster; that the Word was there when God's Messiah, King Cyrus, "saved" Israel out of Babylon; that the Word was what Paul heard on the Damascus Road.

So when this man says, "I AM the light of the world," he is revealing to our sight—"incarnating," if you like—what is eternal reality, namely, that God in the beginning had *said* the Word "Light," and there was light (Gen. 1:3).

When this man says, "You are the light of the world," he is revealing the corporate nature of what it means to be Son of Man; for he invited all those who are now one *with* him in the Covenant to share *with* him in God's saving work.

When this man says, "I AM the Way" (with probable reference to Prov. 8:22—"the way God creates"), "the Truth" (that is to say, Ultimate Reality), "and the Life" (that is to say, what God is)—for God in the Old Testament is the *living* God—then John shows us Jesus revealing to us mere creatures of a day how he has brought into our lives these three ultimates that belong to God alone—but always in terms of function and not of essence.

Despite what may appear to us on a superficial reading of Jesus' words "I AM" to reflect a kind of triumphalism, it was only when people saw Jesus in the light of God's revelation of himself as the great I AM who had descended with Israel into the "hell" of Babylon that the tremendous significance of that great name could come home to them. During the Exile Deutero-Isaiah had discovered the "strange" reality (to use the word Isaiah employed at Isa. 28:21) that God "worked" in a fashion that no man on earth had ever dreamed of before, and so, of course, as no other god had done, for the gods were the product of the thoughts and perceptions of man. When Israel had been in depths of despair, and when all human values and religious aspirations seemed to be but vanity— vanity of vanities—it was this "voice," who had shared this existential nihilism with his fellows, who revealed to us a first glimpse of the final reality. Moreover, the voice records how this glimpse came from the lips of pagans and not of the covenant people: "God is *in* you only," they declared in astonishment, "and there is no other, no god besides him." To which follows the postscript, "Truly thou art a God who hidest thyself, O God of Israel, the Savior"—the God who hides himself, not *in* the mysteries of philosophical speculation, not in the problem of pain and suffering, of earthquakes, wind, and fire, but—*in* Israel! The Husband had so identified himself with his Bride (as pagans recognized before Israel saw it herself) that he who is Spirit had hidden himself in her who is mere human flesh. As gender is only an accident of what it means to be flesh, we can speak of Israel as either God's servant (masculine) or his "handmaiden of low estate" (the feminine form of the same word; see Luke 1:48). And so, as we have seen already, God's answer to the destruction in 587 B.C. of all human values, human hopes, human religions, and human civilizations was to empty himself *in* Israel and thus to share with his Bride the totally negative task of being the suffering servant.

In the year 740 B.C. Isaiah went through a conversion experience. Till that time he had obviously thought, as religious man naturally thinks, that God can do all things, in that he is the Almighty. God has only to will his will, and with a sweep of his arm he can bring in the victory. Isaiah went through a transforming experience, however, as we read in Isaiah 6. In all sincerity as a young man he entered the Temple to pray, and there and then he had what we would call a religious experience. That is to say, something happened to him that he had not chosen for himself. God confronted Isaiah with his awful holiness, before which Isaiah knew himself to be as nothing. "Woe is me!" he cried, "for I am 'lost'." This word might well be translated by "taken to pieces," "be made to disintegrate into negation." This is of course what sin does to a person; it removes him from the realm of God to belonging to the people known as sons of Belial, people who are intent on destruction, whereas God always works at reconstruction. There is no in between way. As Revelation 3:16 puts it: "Because you are lukewarm, and neither cold nor hot, I will spew you out of my mouth." Yet here we encounter the immense paradox that it is the way of *de*struction that God chooses in the case of this man Isaiah at this turning point in his life.

But the destruction is only the first step to reconstruction. God now recreates Isaiah, something he cannot do for himself. He does this by forgiving him for his sin. Isaiah is now integrated; God has made him a man of *integrity*. What then must he preach about God? The answer, terrible as it seems to be at first hearing, is in line with what Isaiah himself has just experienced at the hand of God. Isaiah has to preach doom, he has to preach the utter end of all human hopes and strivings, he has to preach even that man will refuse to accept the fact that of himself he is nothing. He has to preach so as to compel people to shut their ears and close their eyes to the basically pagan view that man creates his own gods, man controls his own life, and man can save his own soul as well as his own culture and society. But his preaching is to go beyond even that. He must create the total alienation of Israel from God, even though Israel is the chosen people, chosen by God to be his instrument.

The key to understanding this terrible message, however, is to be found in the very last clause of the chapter. So incongruous does this short line seem to be that it is only those scholars who have sought to penetrate to an understanding of what God calls his "strange" ways who reject the idea that these last few words are a later addition and do not come from Isaiah. They are, "The holy seed is its stump." In these words the RSV renders the phrase correctly. The TEV has paraphrased its meaning clearly. The NEB has produced only a nonsense line.

In the year 1945 Professor Joseph L. Hromadka of Czechoslovakia wrote a slim volume entitled *Doom and Resurrection* (S.C.M. Press). He wrote as one who, like Deutero-Isaiah, had to experience from within the collapse of all hopes and values and human and social aspirations. For he knew from within what it meant for Czechoslovakia to be conquered, overrun, and then harshly subdued by a cruel foe. Many theologians in the safety of the West were uneasy and unbelieving about what he wrote then. In fact, since the Second World War, many theologians have completely failed to understand the thesis of Hromadka's book. Hromadka stood beside Isaiah of old. There cannot be life as God has planned it, he declared shortly, without there first being an end to all man's futile religions, philosophies, and social reconstructions. There can be resurrection, reconstruction, recreation only through and out of the Cross. "The holy seed is its stump." "The blood of the martyrs is the seed of the church." In other words, the sermon given to Isaiah to preach was in fact in tune with the gospel that we discover in the New Testament.

We turn back now to note at what moment the centurion made his cry, "Truly this man was the Son of God." It was not when men shouted sarcastically, "Save yourself and come down from the cross," hoping to observe a great champion, a ruler of men, a messianic figure, leap down in triumph, like a heavyweight boxer shaking hands with himself above his head. It was not when the crowds poured out to hear the famous preacher speaking on the shores of the Lake and then sought to make him king. It was not when, as men expected him to, Jesus answered Pilate word for word, sarcasm for sarcasm, philosophical jibe for philosophical jibe; it was at that moment when he was nothing, when he was emptied out, not having the strength even to suck a sponge filled with a tart, refreshing vinegar, abandoned, it would seem, by both God and man. It was when this Jesus was finished, dead, a mere bleeding carcass. Yet it was then, paradoxically, that the centurion's insight gave God the chance to demonstrate finally and uniquely that Doom must precede Resurrection.

What a strange God this is, this God of Isaiah of old. How utterly other he is than Allah, or Krishna, or the gods of the mystics of Islam, or Buddhism, or Christianity itself, or Baha'i or Theosophy, or anything else. This figure was no charismatic or messianic leader of men as he groaned out his life on the Cross. This was no hero, like a Greek god or man striding through the pages of history, no Napoleon, no Buddha, no Sun Myung Moon, no glittering California impresario, raising millions of dollars in his preaching campaign—not even a Thomas Aquinas, or a John Knox, or a Cardinal Manning. This was a mere nobody, a nothing; and so we are not at all surprised to read that on the last night of his life "They all ran away and left him."

Yet stranger still is the reality of that utter negation which is signified by the Cross of Christ. For it is that which is *the* power of God to change, to recreate people's hearts, to transform the evils of human society, and to overcome the mystery of evil itself in this strange natural world. Thus the negation of the Cross is absolutely other than the negation of *Nirvana*. For *Nirvana* marks the end. But, like the holy seed that is present in the stump, even when the tree has been felled to the ground, it is *at that point* of action that resurrection takes place, that new life comes forth, that the new creation begins.

Jesus was a teacher. But his teaching served only as an interpretation of his activity as the "emptied-out servant." His teaching was always explication of the Word that God had already given to Israel, especially that Word as it is expressed in the Prologue to the Bible. There is therefore no place for Jesus to be hung in the gallery of the great teachers of the world.

In the short space allotted we can take up only one area of this relation between teaching and action. In parables of word and action Jesus interprets the eternal creativity of God over against what we might call three disaster areas of human life, three areas that incarnate the chaos that has been present in the world since the beginning. We might even call these three culprits the unholy trinity of defiant evil.

In Luke 13:4-5 Jesus teaches how God handles natural disasters. He uses as an illustration the collapse of the tower of Siloam, which killed 18 innocent people. His teaching on this particular event can of course be extended by implication to all disasters, such as earthquakes, floods, hurricanes, fires, and storms at sea.

Second, in Luke 13:1-3 Jesus teaches how God handles the inherent cruelty in human nature. Men have sacked Jerusalem, Nineveh, Rome, and Dresden as well as most other cities of the world. Men have carried on a slave trade in human beings throughout the ages. Men today torture independent thinkers in mental hospitals and police stations, and dismiss them to work themselves to death in salt mines and Siberian hells on earth. By so doing men reveal their basic egotism, pride, sadism, and fear.

In John 9:2 Jesus handles the third "disaster area" of human experience, that of pain and suffering and the frailty of human flesh. It is the story of how Jesus healed the man born blind. The three disaster areas thus comprehend the "one whole reality of chaos," as we human beings experience life on earth. We recall how God set off this "whole," which he called Night, but to which he gave the right to exist by giving it a name. He separated it from the area to which he also gave a name, that of Day. Yet he bound the two together to form "one new whole reality," "one day" of both darkness and light, as Genesis 1:5 puts it pictorially.

It is to this Genesis passage that Jesus refers his hearers in all three situations. He does so by revealing God as working in him in the same way God has done since the beginning of creation. Adherents of the Eastern religions seek an escape from suffering, from the reality that Day and Night are bound together as one day. Jesus reveals, however, that God accepts the world as it is, with good and evil all bound up together, "one day." Thus God accepts each seemingly unimportant human situation, each little human "day," and then acts to bring forth a new situation that now belongs, not in the kingdom of Satan, but, to use Jesus' own language, in the kingdom of the Son.

A lady doctor married very happily late in life. Though she was 43 years of age she was determined to have a child, believing that this was God's will for herself and her husband. She knew the risks of childbearing at her age. Thus when her baby was born a mongol, there were those who called her a fool. But her comment as she gazed on her severely handicapped little boy was: "Never shall a baby receive as much love as we shall give this baby." She could make this loving declaration because she and her husband had already been rescued from the kingdom of Satan and were now living in the kingdom of Christ. "My kingdom is not of this world," Jesus had said. This kingdom displayed that new love which had been *created* out of the pain, sorrow, horror, and even sheer wickedness of the world as we know it.

It is a sad feature of the world of both dogmatic and systematic theology that it frequently shows ignorance of, if not indifference to, biblical theology. No one should work in the area of soteriology who is unaware of the Hebrew terms that the Old Testament employs to describe God's saving actions.

Let us take, then, this verb "to save." The root is *y-sh-ʿ*, used normally in the Hiphil, the active, transitive form of the verb. From it two nouns derive, both of which are translated by the English word "salvation." The first noun for salvation is *yeshaʿ*. This noun describes what God has done for us. "The Lord brought us up out of the land of Egypt, out of slavery." He has "delivered" us, "rescued" us, "redeemed" us, "ransomed" us—all verbs that like *y-sh-ʿ* are used to describe God's initial action. Once God has done this for us, we are "saved." At least that is how certain types of popular evangelists like to think of God's saving activity. God has "converted" us, so that we are *now converted*. We are now living in a state of salvation. We are now "Christians." But this view of the meaning of salvation can be taken only in defiance of biblical language.

For there is a second noun form deriving from the root *y-sh-ʿ*. This one appears in the feminine, namely, *teshuʿah*. We cannot blame the revivalist preacher for not noting the difference between the two nouns, for the KJV itself has been unaware of it. But then, much scholarly work has been done since 1611! Paul, however, who knew his Hebrew, drew a clear distinction between the two nouns.

When God acts to save a person, what he is doing is to continue his basic activity in his eternal capacity as Creator. In bestowing his love on the sinner and in forgiving him, God has produced a new thing, a new creation, what Paul calls "the new man in Christ." This new man is new because he has been rescued from loving and worshipping himself, from seeking and searching for his own salvation. He has been motivated now to the business of loving and worshipping God. But the reality is, as we must recognize, that the forgiven sinner remains a sinner—*simul justus ac peccator*, as Martin Luther put it. Even the person who can name the date and hour of his conversion is not yet "a Christian" in the biblical view. He is still in need of the second half of God's saving activity in his life, known to Isaiah as God's *teshu'ah*. It is interesting to recognize certain unifying factors in the long book of Isaiah, covering, as it does, the years 740 B.C. to about 500 B.C., and written, as it was, by a number of persons. Isaiah of Jerusalem, about whose call and conversion we read in Isaiah 6, was the first to make full use of the two concepts described by the nouns *yesha'* and *teshu'ah*; all the successive writers in his school, as well as the later psalmists, followed his lead.

Teshu'ah is also an action of God. After a person is "saved," "converted," God gives him the initiative and the power to love others, the strength and the commitment necessary to *create* new lives in other people. Perhaps this may be done only through deep suffering, as Isaiah discovered only *after* he had confessed his conversion—as we see in the second half of Isaiah 6. It is pathetic to meet youngsters in this generation who say "We are born-again Christians" but whose basic concern still seems to be that of caring for and nurturing their own souls. "This is my commandment, that you love one another as I have loved you." How has he loved me? By emptying himself even of his rightful claim to be the Son of God, by laying down his life for his friends. And when we recall that in the Old Testament the words "life" and "soul" are one, then we are moved to astonishment at the claim that the word *teshu'ah* lays on us. The Christian is not one who can merely say "I am born again," that is, recreated by God, for that reality is only covered by the masculine word. The Christian is he whom others can see has *also* been empowered to empty himself of his ego, and so to pour out his "soul," even as Christ did, thus becoming the servant of others even to the end of the earth (Isa. 49:6).

Parallel with the two nouns for "salvation" are two others, both translated by our word "righteousness." The root is *ṣ-d-q*, meaning "to be right," or "to be in the right."

Consequently the active, transitive form of the verb means "to put right." In theological usage, therefore, it means "to be put right with God," "to be brought into a right relationship with God." So the masculine noun refers to this action of God. This is, of course, the work of God alone. The feminine noun, consequently, must also be the work of God alone. It means—and we can only paraphrase—"the power to be so concerned for others that one seeks to bring them into a right relationship with God." It is that state of blessedness to which Jesus refers when he declares "Blessed are the *shalom*-makers," *not* "those who live in peace with God and man." That is a Buddhist blessedness, not a Christian one. The relationship between the masculine and the feminine nouns is expressed clearly in an easy-to-grasp metaphor that we find at Isaiah 45:8.

The biblical concept of salvation, therefore, is not limited to the idea of "finding salvation," as in the East. It must include within it acceptance of God's power to empty oneself that others, too, may be saved. Thus one is not "saved" until, by God's power, he or she has done just that.

Fëdor Dostoevsky once wrote: "What is hell? I maintain that it is the suffering of being unable to love." Even the "born-again Christian," therefore, is still in hell unless he has allowed God to grant him *teshu'ah*, too. It is a pity that few modern translations of the Psalms have been successful in expressing the joy of the Psalmist when he says "thank you" to God for that unspeakable divine gift.

Jesus was a teacher, yes indeed. He was also a prophet, a rabbi, and much more. These are all aspects of his being a man. Yet all the titles given him are subsidiary to his being, not just a man, but the Servant *par excellence*. Jesus was not even a moralist. He could leave that area of his teaching to the Pharisees. He had taught about the love of God that creates new situations. But his being the world's Servant was the "way" in which God let loose in the world this creative love of his. He did not do so by strong human leadership, or by clever philosophical teaching, or by an evident charismatic power. God's power of love was let loose particularly at that moment when Jesus told Judas to go and do the evil thing he had planned to do, and then added, in tune with what he had said of the three "disaster areas" we have noted, "*Now* is the Son of man glorified, and in him God is glorified"(John 13:31).

The glory of God is God's creative love made visible. Some of the Psalmists suggested that one could almost see this happen, and so they spoke of it as being like a garment that God wore. But the glory of God becomes visible, becomes incarnate, when the blind see, when the blood of the martyrs becomes the seed of the church, when the individual discovers the blessedness of being able to forgive those who sin against him, or when he has had to live through a shattering natural disaster and found that God had been there *with* him in all that he had had to suffer. But more than all, we see the glory of God at that extraordinary moment when Jesus quoted Psalm 22 aloud as he hung in agony on the Cross.

The first words of the psalm are "My God, my God, why hast thou forsaken me?" Yet we know that before he died Jesus surrendered his life to God in total commitment, because he also quoted the last words of the psalm. This fact has led scholars to suggest that Jesus used the whole psalm as an expression of faith; if so, then he also uttered a line in the middle of it, "I am a worm, and no man" (v. 6). We should not forget that God had already called the Israel with whom Jesus had identified himself at his baptism a worm, through the lips of Deutero-Isaiah, as the latter experienced the humiliation of the Exile (Isa. 41:14). Could any word more profoundly express the abyss of suffering that Jesus had to undergo than this? The Son of Man was no man after all, but only a worm.

The Creed puts it: "He descended into hell." We have already noted that we are to understand eternity eschatologically in that it is virtually created by each *now* through which we live here in space and time. So Jesus knew what separation from God meant when on the Cross he made his cry; that is what hell surely is, separation from the living God, and knowing it. But eternity is quite other than time. Eternity is yesterday as well as tomorrow. That surely is why the last book of the New Testament can speak of Jesus on the Cross as "the Lamb slain from the foundation of the world."

How shortsighted it is, then, to speak of Jesus as "The

Founder of Christianity." This puts him on a par with the gods of the Hindu pantheon. In the same way, it is equally shortsighted to suggest that the Church was born at Pentecost. Jesus did not found a church, he found one, one that had been created by God himself out of the dead bones of Israel five hundred years before the Christchild was born in Bethlehem.

The religion known as Judaism, along with Christianity, has its origin at that moment in the dawn of human self-consciousness when "men began to call upon the name of the Lord" (Gen. 4:26). But it is Christianity alone that has recognized the strange new thing God did, even as that "voice" whom we call Deutero-Isaiah has explained to us, when God made himself one flesh *with* and *in* Israel. And he has become in her that Suffering Servant who is the total opposite of the gods and heroes of man whom the world has admired and followed in both East and West ever since the dawn of history.

CHAPTER 10

The Church Is Mission

*H*AVING BEEN A MISSIONARY MUCH OF MY LIFE I AM
frequently invited to speak on "The Church and
Missions." This, of course, I refuse to do; I agree to accept the
invitation only if my title can be "The Church Is Mission." We
must naturally look for the biblical evidence for such a
dogmatic statement.

It is interesting to discover in our day, having as we do an
intimate knowledge of all the countries of the world, that
ancient Israel believed that there were 70 nations on the
earth. To reach that figure they had evidently made use of
Babylonian material. The list they drew up is recorded now in
the tenth chapter of Genesis. It is the so-called Table of
Nations, and it represents the descendants of Noah through
his three sons, Shem, Ham, and Japheth. Whether the list is
historically accurate or not does not matter to us today. For
example, the ancient Near East could not possibly have
known of the Japanese or Eskimo peoples. Again, perhaps
through a scribal addition made at some period in the
transmission of the text, it is possible to discover 71 names
rather than the 70 that would be the original number. At least,
70 is the number the early scribes had in mind. For Genesis 10
was written for a theological purpose and was not meant to be
a textbook in geography. Then again, the name of Israel is not
to be found in the list.

However, quite a different source leads us to believe that
the Israel that came out of Egypt was composed of 70 clans
(see the word *nephesh*—Exod. 1:5). Really what we have is
"70 heads of extended families," for Israel did its numbering
in that way, just as the people of Polynesia do today. This

tradition is found also in that very ancient poem to which we have already alluded, the Song of Moses (Deut. 32:8). There we read:

> *When the Most High gave to the nations their inheritance,*
> *   when he separated the sons of men,*
> *he fixed the bounds of the peoples*
> *   according to the number of the sons of Israel.*

This means that from earliest times Israel recognized that her election had a theological significance in relation to the rest of humanity. Moreover, this relationship reveals why Israel is not just one of the nations, number 71 if you like. Israel dare not forget that she is elect to be a kingdom of priests to the rest of the world. That same verse in Deuteronomy speaks of Israel as being "the Lord's portion, his allotted heritage." But since Israel was in covenantal relationship with the Lord, it meant that Israel was elect to do what God does, with God working through her and in her.

Naturally it took centuries for the meaning of Israel's election to sink into their sinful heads. The great prophets are sufficient witness to that. Actually it never did sink in, just as it does not sink into the mind of the average member of the Christian Church today. There are Christians today who suppose that they are "elect to be saved," and thus to escape the fires of hell. They think this way despite the words of Jesus: "He who seeks to save his soul [or life—they can be the same word in Hebrew] will lose it." It was our "voice" again, in the bonds of exile, who made the reason for Israel's election explicit: "I will give you as a light to the nations, that my salvation may reach to the end of the earth" (Isa. 49:6).

Somewhere around 300 B.C. the decision was made to translate the Torah, the name given to the first five books of the Old Testament, into Greek. The translation of the other books of the Old Testament was made later. The decision was made at that time because, while the tiny Israelite nation knew the Hebrew language, no one else of all the 70 nations of the earth could understand it. The Greek language, on the other hand, was the "world" language of the day, the "ecumenical" language of the Mediterranean basin and far to the East. We know nothing of the circumstances surrounding the making of the translation, although we hear legends about what happened. This translation into Greek came to be known as the Septuagint, this being the Latin word for 70. Setting aside the legends, we notice that later generations came to call this translation "The Book of the 70," the book telling of God and his creative plan for the world and meant to be given to all the nations.

Both Jesus and his disciples clearly held this conviction. For no one considered it odd when he sent 70 Israelites out on mission. He did not send 67 or 73, nor did he send Greeks, or Romans, or Egyptians (Luke 10:1-12). It appears that Jesus was demonstrating that God's covenant with Israel still stood, and that Israel was the instrument God still planned to use for the evangelization of the world. To make this emphasis in still another way, Jesus chose 12 apostles—not 10, not 16. The word "apostle" simply means "missionary." By so doing he was demonstrating that his mission was the same as that of the 12 tribes of Israel. Each of these 12 apostles, these "heads of extended families," was of course a male. The symbolism Jesus used would have been obscured, of course, if he had included even one woman. So now, this chosen band was elect to minister to the 70 nations of the world, certainly not to expect to be ministered to by it. We recall the hard message that Isaiah as a young man was given to preach (Isa. 6:9–13). He had experienced that forgiveness of God which can give a man the deepest satisfaction and sense of blessedness. Yet he did not ask for a continual outpouring of the Spirit, which some Christians today think is the biblical thing to do. What he did without any hesitation was to say, "Here am I, send me." To be a Christian is to be a missionary.

We dare to declare that Israel *is* mission on the ground that God himself is mission, as Israel discovered through her covenantal relationship with him. We have already employed "biblical mathematics" to illustrate the nature of the sending of Israel. Now we use another biblical illustration to show the mission of God himself. This is the way in which the Bible uses the figure of angels.

The word "angel" in the two biblical languages means

"messenger," that is, one sent on a mission. The messenger's task is to convey a message from God to man. And since God is conceivable only in personal terms, the messenger must be personal, too. Thus the messenger, the angel, is always portrayed as a human being, usually as a young man, even as Jesus himself was a young man. Angels are never depicted as having wings, despite the stained glass windows in medieval churches and despite all the paintings in Italian galleries. We are to remember that the seraphim and the cherubim (-*im* being the Hebrew plural ending) are not angels. Angels are *sent* by God, they are God's *mission*. But God does not send seraphim. These creatures represent rather what the Bible means by "religion." While the word "religion" does not occur in the Bible, the idea of religion does, in this picture form. The nearest likeness to that of the seraphim has come down to us as the Sphinx in Egypt, a kind of lion squatting on its haunches, its serpent's tail hidden beneath it, its wings folded, gazing at us with a human face—not very different from some of the gods of India today. The seraphim that young Isaiah could see in front of him in the Temple had been placed there by a conquering Assyrian king as an act of spite and self-glory. But what Isaiah discovered by God's grace was that these emblems of man's religious concepts were now being used by God to his own glory!

The angel, on the other hand, is the "picture" of the revelation of God's loving plan and purpose for man coming to him in a living manner, because God is the living God. A clear description of such thinking is given in Exodus 23:20. But let us remember that we are reading "picture theology."

We listen to God speaking to Moses: "See," says God (i.e., "Don't forget that what follows is a mental picture delivered at the level of your simple human understanding"). "See, with your mind's eye, that *I* [very emphatic] am sending a 'mission' ahead of you"—surely a beautiful way of speaking of prevenient grace. God lets us "see" grace, so that we do not need to argue about it philosophically. The next verse then expresses the living nature of the mission, alive even as God himself is the living God: "To guard you on the way, and to bring you to the place which I have prepared." This sentence tells us about God, not about the nature of angels, just as when Jesus says, "I go to prepare a place for you." The text continues: "Don't repulse him, else he won't forget your rebelliousness. I declare that my Person is in him." But surely, we exclaim, only God who can forgive sins! Yes indeed, but remember that the angel is no less than the Person of God present at that moment when he becomes active in Israel's experience.

What we have here, then, expresses the mystery that, in sending his angel, his missionary, God is present *in* his messenger, yet remains God above. What God sends is his Self. So it comes as no surprise, when we leap to the last words of Matthew's Gospel, to hear the risen Christ declare: "I shall be *with* you always, even to the end of the world." I shall be with you in your mission of making disciples of all nations.

CHAPTER 11

Jesus and the World's Religions

SO WE RETURN ONCE AGAIN TO OUR QUESTION: WHAT IS TO BE
our relationship to those neighbors of ours who sincerely
hold to one or other of the world's great religions?

First, we are to remember that these are indeed real
religions. The Muslim unashamedly spreads his prayer mat in
his place of work before the eyes of his workmates, prostrates
himself, and prays toward Mecca even in working hours. On
the other hand, the Muslim's religious zeal may take another
form, a form not very different from the fanaticism of the
Crusades to the Holy Land at the end of the Middle Ages.
Lytton Strachey writes of the Muslim armies of the Mahdi in
the Sudan a hundred years ago: "The brazen war-drums
would summon, with their weird rolling, the whole host to
arms. The great army would move forward, coloured,
glistening, dark, violent, proud, beautiful. The drunkenness,
the madness, of religion would blaze on every face; and the
Mahdi, immovable on his charger, would let the scene grow
under his eyes in silence."

The Hindu may sing a devotional and very personal
hymn such as Professor Hick quotes in his book *God Has
Many Names*, one that closely resembles the pietist hymnol-
ogy of some seventeenth-century German Anabaptists, or of a
modern sect in California. Or our Sikh neighbor may be glad
to tell us about what he so greatly values in his religion, with
its deep moral feeling and concern for what is good and just.

A real religion is a total way of life. Sir Edmund Hillary,
of Mount Everest fame, tells how modern Western money-
worshipping visitors have done much to destroy the way of
life of the Sherpas whom he is seeking to help enter the new

world that has opened up to them. This is because so many of the Westerners who invade the mountains are not Christians, but mere humanists, and often dogmatically so. A true Hindu or Christian would respect the Sherpa way of life. A real religion rules not just a man's worship, but also his politics, his morals, his home life, his social customs, his "universe of thought." Because of this it is extremely difficult for an individual to "convert" from one real religion to another. To do so may mean that he has to break with custom, morality, family, and state. The resurgence of fundamentalist Islam in our time makes this quite plain to even the most obtuse Christian. Moreover, the saying, "No man is an island," applies not just to Christian believers but to adherents of all religions. Consequently it might even be cruel (and therefore quite unChristlike) to seek to make an individual cut himself off from the total world view in which he has been reared and to which he is now totally adjusted.

Such an act is known as proselytism, something quite distinct from evangelism. In Matthew 23:15 we hear Jesus' rejection of such activity: "Woe to you, scribes and Pharisees, hypocrites! for you traverse sea and land to make a single proselyte, and when he becomes a proselyte, you make him twice as much a child of hell as yourselves." That is to say, you insist on his losing the degree of *shalom* he knew when he fitted into the context of his own faith. If he breaks with his old pattern of experience he may become a mere disengaged individual who cannot find his place in the *shalom* of the Christian community.

On the other hand, it is a mistake to say, as some "World Faith" protagonists do, that God is as truly worshipped by Muslims, theistic Hindus, and Amida Buddhists as he is by Christians of any sort. The illogicality of such a statement becomes obvious when we look at the nature of the God who is being worshipped. For there are even sect-like Christian groups whose strange concept of God induces an equally strange worship of God. Nor is it enough for a Christian to declare that he possesses a Christ-figure whom he keeps before his eyes, one that he has worked out for himself and which now completely meets his spiritual needs. The God of the Bible is not there to meet people's spiritual needs. Rather, he is there to accost us with his love and to challenge us to obedience as he challenged Isaiah. Thus the reality of the revealed nature of God is all important for our discussion of this issue.

In light of that, there are at least three Eastern myths or figures that the Christian must necessarily reject. One is the ancient figure of the mountain. This figure declares that there are many paths up the mountain of God. There is the Christian path, a Muslim path, a Theosophist path, a Baha'i path, and so on. These may in fact all follow different routes, but they all meet eventually at the top. The second myth is the Buddhist figure of the three monkeys—hear no evil, see no evil, speak no evil. Negation such as that has no place in the biblical revelation. The third myth enshrines the idea that man is meant to go in search of God. Theosophy, a Westernized form of Hinduism, requires a journey in search of the divine (if one of its adherents has informed me correctly) that lasts all of 16 years. The biblical revelation, on the contrary, is that there is no need for any journey in search of God, either up a mountain or over a lifetime of years; for God has already made the journey to us—in creative love, loyalty, and self-emptying service. Thus the Christian revelation allows man to give up all those forms of selfish seeking for salvation which are a basic element in the religions of the East.

We have consistently used the words "creative love" in this biblical theological essay. These two English words are our attempt to translate that Hebrew feminine term for salvation which we examined in Chapter 9. I believe that the content of the New Testament Greek words for love must allow for this Old Testament usage; for its significance was hammered out in the historical experience of the people of Israel. From this it follows that the Christian word "love" does not mean what others think it means. One of India's foremost theologians told a class of mine that "Hinduism and Christianity actually meet in that both believe that love is God." Politeness dictated that I wait till he had concluded his lecture before pointing out to him that there is no such thing as love. Love is merely an abstract idea. Love exists only when there is *someone* who loves. For love is an activity. Thus the Christian could not agree that love is God. He must declare that God is love, for only the love of a Lover can recreate the personality of another. We read of Jesus, that when he was confronted by a poor blind man he *looked* at him—a very deep and searching activity indeed—and *loved* him, then his *bowels moved* inside him, and finally he *touched* him. This is, of course, an echo of what Hosea, in the eleventh chapter of his book, had already said of God: "When Israel was a child, I loved him, and out of Egypt I called my son. . . . It was I who taught Ephraim to walk (by touching and holding him), I took them up in my arms. . . . How can I give you up, O Ephraim! . . . My *heart is turned over on top of me*, my compassion flames up"(slightly paraphrased!). Such, then, is how we are to understand the words "God is love," and discover that, if that is his name, it is a different name from that of any other god.

Again, the biblical concept of God does not express the idea of love in a merely philosophical sense. God's love is not only for man, it is also for his inanimate creation, for matter. During the Second World War the British Broadcasting Corporation conducted a series of talks entitled "People Matter." Whereupon that great figure, Archbishop William Temple, asked whether he could give an extra talk entitled "Things Matter." The biblical God loves things. His ultimate aim is to create "new heavens and a new *earth*"—matter, if you like. Moreover, this he has already begun to do. The New Testament does not speak of the resuscitation of Jesus' body, as in the case of Lazarus, or of the survival of Jesus' "soul" on Easter Day. It proclaims that God resurrected the whole Son of Man, "warts and all." God's action was to raise to himself the matter that forms the body of a human creature. As John Calvin put it: "God became man, that man might become God." And he did so in conformity with his promise to Israel of old. God had included "the land" as one element, one strand, in the total skein of promises that the New Testament declares were fulfilled in Christ. Jesus' body was built up from the land. Everything he had eaten had grown out of the land. Human beings *are* what they eat. This Son of Man, whose body now represented the land of promise, had become, to use Paul's language, the "first-fruits of the new heavens and the new *earth*." The scope of God's creative love surely far exceeds the philosophical ideas found in the world's religions, for these are concerned only with the things of the spirit.

Again, the biblical view of God's love is that it is "good." That word, too, must not be understood in a moral or a philosophical or a "comparative religions" sense. When God created the sun, moon, and stars, the fish, the animals, and the birds, what we read is: "And God saw that it was good." The Hebrew word *tov* is one that is potent with movement and action. The animals of course are not morally good. The sentence means, "And God saw that creation was *good for* his purposes." In English one must always add the preposition *for* to the word "good" in the Bible. When baby Moses was only ten minutes old, his mother saw that he was *tov*. Not morally, surely, nor was he good-looking at that age! No, this strange little creature was good *for* God's plan, as his mother, just like Jesus' mother, was able to declare in a prophetic spirit. God's love is good *for* his world in a manner that other religions have never begun to grasp.

Until a generation ago a large percentage of all the hospitals in India and most of the social work done from them were maintained by the Christian Church, even though it comprised only 2% of the population of India. Then movements arose within Hinduism that sought to copy the Christian *action* in India, even the creation of the YMHA. Today the government of India shares fully in the training of doctors and in the spread of health services, as any developed nation must do. But, as the head of a Christian medical school in North India reminds us, it is difficult to motivate Hindu medical students, on graduation, to take posts in the vast area of India's needy villages. Most graduates hope rather to practice among the rich in a city like Bombay. In this they are not much different from many post-Christian students in Western countries. In other words, neither has recognized that the Christian conception of the word "good" means to be *good for* this needy world. Again, the God whom Mother

Teresa of Calcutta worships and serves is not the God who is worshipped by the Hindu people under whatever name they choose.

Finally, then, to answer the question we raised at the beginning of this chapter, I would suggest that the Christian individual or congregation should keep the following issues in mind:

(1) It is only right that we should seek to know our new neighbor, and to understand what his religion—this most important area of his life—is all about. Most of us take for granted that the other man must be basically "just like me." We should do our neighbor the courtesy of studying the religion that is the very basis of his life.

(2) We should encourage our congregations to take a fresh look at our own preconceptions as to what the Christian Faith means. Clearly, the study of other people's beliefs will help us all "to see ourselves as others see us." It may be, for example, that we shall find ourselves being led to discover what is really central to the Christian Faith when we observe the personal piety of our Hindu neighbor. It may be that only when we find a good Hindu (but what does "good" mean?) doing much the same thing as we do, that we shall begin to see that personal piety is not the central element in Christianity.

(3) We must remember that the Judaeo-Christian faith is the only religion in the world to express itself in terms of covenant. Some Old Testament scholars today are playing down the emphasis on covenant in the Old Testament that earlier scholars have seen to be so important. They do so because the great prophets seem to have little to say about it. But all Old Testament writers have plenty to say about circumcision. Circumcision is the *sign* of the Covenant, and is therefore not a mere "idea" like the idea of covenant, but something that belongs in the realm of human experience. So, too, with the New Testament Covenant. Little is said of it in its pages, but much is said of its *sign*, which is baptism. We can live our lives in faith without constantly keeping in mind that we have been baptized. But Christ gave us a second sacramental sign, his "Supper," to reinforce the significance of our baptism.

When we began our study of I AM, we noticed that God is the God of action. Next we saw that membership in the Old Testament Covenant also required action, in that Israel was to be a light to lighten the Gentiles, and the vehicle of God's saving love to the end of the earth. Consequently, in the case of the New Testament sacraments, too, Jesus asks for action. He says, "Take, eat." Moreover, it is not just bread that we are to eat, it is bread that has been broken that we are summoned to make into one flesh with our physical frame. Nor is the cup the sacramental sign of blood alone; rather it is blood that has been poured out in death that we are meant to make part of ourselves. This is the verb used of the Servant at Isaiah 53:12, where we read, "He poured out his life (or soul) to death."

God is mission; Israel is mission; Christ is mission; therefore we, too, must be mission to the peoples of the earth, not by any triumphalist means, not by seeking to proselytize them, but, with Christ dwelling *in* us, even as God was *in* Israel in exile, by pouring ourselves out in love for and in service to them.

A sentence frequently heard from the lips of a pious Muslim is "In the name of Allah, the Merciful and the Compassionate." Arabic, as a Semitic language, is closely related to Hebrew. The two adjectives used in this declaration of faith derive from the one root, *r-ḥ-m*. We find it used by our "voice" in Exile, for whom it means womb or belly. Thus at times it may carry the overtone of that depth of painful, creative mother-love which no male can ever experience. God addresses "the remnant of the house of Israel, who have been borne by me from your birth, carried from the womb (*r-ḥ-m*)," as we read at Isaiah 46:3. At 49:15 he asks, "Can a woman forget her sucking child, that she should have no compassion on the son of her womb? Even these may forget, yet I will not forget you."

The Greek equivalent of this Hebrew verb is used of Jesus in the Gospels, as we have seen already, in that "his insides were turned upside down within him." So what of "In the name of Allah"? The "name," as we recall, means a picture of its owner. Is it not our duty to give that name a face, if we believe we have seen it? And should we not let our

Muslim neighbor see this kind of compassion on the face of the Son of Man? In doing so we can remind our Muslim friend that this Son of Man is mentioned in the Quran, at Sura 4:169 and elsewhere, where we read that *'Isa* (Jesus) was the Messiah, born of a virgin, that he was God's *'ila* (Word), and that he was *a spirit from God*. I, too, firmly believe that Muhammad was God's prophet, as every Muslim affirms. But he was a prophet who was unable to recognize that the Word which he spoke was once crucified and emptied out into death.

Joshua Heschel, the great modern interpreter of Judaism, points out that biblical history bears witness to the constant corruption of man. So bad is he that except for grace there is no hope for him. History is not enough in itself, he says, for it needs "the end of the days." Earlier in this essay I suggested that Christianity in embryo diverged from Judaism in embryo at the time of Israel's exile in Babylon. One has only to read the many interpretations of the sacrifice of the Servant of Isaiah 53 from Jewish pens to be aware of the division between us. The Aramaic Targums, for example, do not attempt to translate literally into that language, the popular speech of the Jewish people of Jesus' day, what is written in the Hebrew. Their writers are consumed with the desire to present the picture of a triumphalist Israel. Heschel sees the falsity of such a misrepresentation of the biblical text. He differs from the Christian only in not seeing that that chapter did actually speak of "the end of the days." So again it is the Cross that forms the stumbling block to the Jew as it does to the Muslim.

The aim of all Hindus is to escape from the wheel of *samsara* (the cyclic time-process, such as that from which Paul helped his Greek hearers escape), and from *karma* itself (the principle of moral reaction applied to both good and evil actions)—escape, release, liberation, emancipation, salvation. Their Hinduism may indeed lead them to all that, but their desire to reach that state is a selfish one. Ought we not therefore invite our Hindu friend and neighbor to discover the joy of finding a means of filling this selfish void with the power of the Cross, and so to live a life of *creative* love—yet

without disturbing the basic culture of his Hindu background?

Shinto is "the way of the Japanese people." Within its
world view the word *kami* means all the natural phenom-
ena—the sun, the mountains, birth, and growth. Educated
Japanese today, however, suggest that these are really
spiritual beings deriving from ancestral spirits. But why
should we not invite our Japanese friends who believe this
way to discover also the realities of forgiveness, freedom, and
eternal life, while remaining good Japanese? God has indeed
not left himself without a witness everywhere. There is a
Shinto proverb which runs, "One kind word can warm three
winter months!" That is fine and good. But does such a
philosophy alone help a man discover the ultimate meaning
of the divine activity?

The Transcendental Meditation taught by Maharishi
Mahesh Yogi is meant to lead to rest and peace *out of* this
world and its problems. Can we not *add* to this hope, so that by
going the way of the Cross we can help transform the world as
it now is?

In all our approaches to people of other faiths or of none,
however, we are to remember that, while all men are of course
under the judgment of God (for all are sinners), the "woes"
Jesus uttered were addressed, not to those outside the
Covenant, but to those within it; for along with great privilege
must always go great responsibility. But even with respect to
the covenant people he died with these words on his lips:
"Father, forgive them; for they know not what they do."

We should note, however, that while there are many
words for sin in the Old Testament, most of them describe
actions that are subsidiary to, or result from, the basic sin of
pesha'. This is a covenantal term; it means rebellion against
one's election to the kingdom of priests. We see clearly what it
signifies when we read the first chapter of Isaiah. The sins of
the Gentiles—murder, adultery, cruelty, rape, greed, and the
rest—are reprehensible indeed, and God's just judgment is
therefore on them, as we see in Amos 1–2. But, as Paul
discovered on the Damascus Road, the rebellion of God's
elect people against living their election, and thus their

kicking against the pricks of God's compulsion to be a light to lighten the Gentiles, is the ultimate sin of the scribes and Pharisees.

"Believing onto Christ," as both the Hebrew and the Greek words have it, means not merely "accepting him as Savior and Lord" in the traditional and accepted form of thinking. It means stepping onto a moving staircase (an application of the vitality and activity of Hebrew thinking!) and being willing to be carried along with it wherever it may go. The judgment of God rests therefore, first and foremost, on those who, having been baptized and therefore members of the Covenant, deliberately elect to step off this escalator and go their own selfish way in life.

But those who stay aboard this onward-moving activity of the living Christ, taking up their cross daily, and "emptying themselves" in love and compassion for their neighbor, find themselves actually enjoying eternal life, beginning here and now. Not only so, but they find themselves imparting that life to those whom they are seeking to serve in love. The whole notion of converting individuals from one "religion" to another has gone with the wind. They are now going with him who *is* eternal life, and they are sharing with him in his work for the salvation of the world by wooing it into fellowship with God. Such people are able to do this only because they have first been with him in the biblical "waste places," represented in our case by the racial ghettos in the slums of our cities. For the racial tensions and dogmatic superiority of one culture and religion over against another are no less than manifestations of the "chaos" that has been present in human life since the foundation of the world. But Christ has also been present in that "chaos," for he is the Lamb slain from the foundation of the world.

Such men and women, then, because they have already been with Christ in the abyss, are in a position to make a positive approach to their possibly shy and bewildered neighbors. We have heard about the latter so often before, from prophet, psalmist, and evangelist alike, for they are known to these authorities as "God's poor." And God's poor have been the object of God's compassion in all ages of humankind.

Consequently, in approaching these "poor," both charity and intellectual argument are rejected. Instead one listens to words such as these: "I know I represent in your eyes the prestige and power of the 'establishment' in this land, perhaps even of an old colonial power. But please don't be afraid either of me or of the frustrations and problems you are meeting at the hands of an unfeeling bureaucracy and of a prejudiced majority of citizens. Remember this, whatever may happen to you, and whatever you may have to face, remember—don't ever forget—'I am with you.' For, you see," we hear the speaker add, "this is the only name of the living God. And since I seek to be his servant, he has allowed me to say that this is my name also: 'I AM with you; this is *my* name for ever.'"

Postscript

PRESENT-DAY ADVOCATES OF RELIGIOUS PLURALISM ("All roads lead eventually to God") remain unaware that it is not possible for a Christian to share their ideas. This is because, quite simply, Christianity is not a religion at all. The word "religion" does not occur in the Bible, except once in the New Testament (KJV) when it a wrong translation of the Greek. Christianity is not just one of the religions of the world, and one of the youngest at that. Its truth rests on historical fact. Thus it is not a philosophy either, nor is it a theosophy. It is based on two facts of history, first on the fact of the "end" of Jerusalem and of God's "chosen people" in 587 B.C., and second on the fact of the Cross of Christ. Moreover, some interreligionists reveal themselves to be so unacquainted with the Bible as to confuse the message of John the Baptist with that of Jesus. For John, the masses are doomed to hell. For Jesus, they are God's "little ones" who desperately need a knowledge of his love and care.

Many educated people in the West believe they are emancipated from "institutional religion," and so from any need to be participants in church life. They declare that they are "grateful to the Church for its civilizing influence on them and their children, for having given them a moral code to live by, and for having kept educational and medical services functioning progressively all throughout the darkest ages of history," to quote a letter-writer to a newspaper. "Just as Paul could say of the old Hebrew faith, 'The law was our schoolmaster to bring us to Christ,' so we can say affectionately of the Christian churches that they have been our schoolmasters to bring us out into the dawning stages of intellectual freedom."

Seven hundred and sixty years before Christ the prophet Amos had proclaimed the message of God: "You only have I known of all the families of the earth; therefore I will punish you for all your iniquities." God's indictment, therefore, is not on this letter-writer for completely misunderstanding the gospel; it is on the Church, its theologians, and its theological colleges and seminaries, for these are the custodians of the gospel. For they have allowed men and women who have been baptized into the Covenant of Grace so to misrepresent the biblical Faith that they can thus publicly disclaim the meaning and the power of the Cross of Christ.